LIVING
THE
PSALMS
LIFE

10 GUIDING PRINCIPLES *for*
FELLOWSHIP *with* GOD

LIVING
THE
PSALMS
LIFE

Dave Branon

Living the Psalms Life: 10 Guiding Principles for Fellowship with God

© 2019 by Dave Branon

Discovery House is affiliated with Our Daily Bread Ministries, Grand Rapids, Michigan.

Requests for permission to quote from this book should be directed to: Permissions Department, Discovery House, PO Box 3566, Grand Rapids, MI 49501, or contact us by email at permissionsdept@dhp.org.

All Scripture quotations, unless otherwise indicated, are taken from the Holy Bible, New International Version®, NIV®. Copyright © 1973, 1978, 1984, 2011 by Biblica, Inc.™ Used by permission of Zondervan. All rights reserved worldwide. zondervan.com. The "NIV" and "New International Version" are trademarks registered in the United States Patent and Trademark Office by Biblica, Inc.™

Interior design by Nicholas Richardson

ISBN: 978-1-62707-921-1

Printed in the United States of America

First printing in 2019

Contents

Introduction

No book of the Bible brings us closer to a more comprehensive view of living than the Psalms. The great reformer Martin Luther called it "a little Bible, wherein everything contained in the entire Bible is beautifully and briefly comprehended."

Luther may have seen it as a "little Bible," but Psalms is still an incredibly long book in its own right, which can make it seem a little daunting for us everyday, normal people.

So we need a bit of help in understanding the principles and teachings of the Psalms—ideas that can help us in our desire to love God more, serve Him better, and grow in our relationship with Him. Because the Psalms are "intended to instruct the mind as well as encourage the heart," as longtime pastor Ray Stedman explained, we want help in learning from this long book the life lessons God has embedded in its pages.[1]

That's the goal of *Living the Psalms Life*. The idea behind the book was to synthesize some of the Psalms' major teachings into ten understandable and usable principles. It's not a complete and comprehensive study of the book; instead it is an attempt to help you see how the Psalms teach us to live in ten specific areas.

For instance, I can't imagine any dedicated believer in Jesus Christ who does not want to live a life that can be called blessed. To have God's smile of approval is high on our spiritual bucket lists. And the book of Psalms gives us some incredibly practical ways to live that kind of life.

As I studied the Psalms in preparation for teaching it at the Adult Bible Fellowship class at my church, I was continually amazed at how practical the teaching of the Psalms is for us in the twenty-first century. It is three-thousand-year-old advice that is as up-to-date as anything you can Google. Plus, the truth and teaching in the Psalms has the undeniable value of coming to us via the Holy Spirit's inspiration.

Whether you've studied the Psalms your whole life or are approaching it for the first time, you'll be challenged by the principles it teaches, and you'll find exciting reality in its practicality.

Living the Psalms Life is more than a title. It is an invitation to explore this amazing book of the Bible and see how it can bring you to new heights of fellowship with God and a new dedication to impacting people whose lives you touch each day.

O n e

The Blessed Life

Shopping in the craft markets in Montego Bay, Jamaica, can be a chore. You step into the marketplace, and you are quickly barraged by kindly yet persistent shopkeepers desperate to show you their wares. Their livelihood depends on getting shoppers—mostly tourists—to spend money on their jewelry, their Jamaica-branded clothes, or a Bob Marley or Usain Bolt memento. Because the need is so great for these hardworking people to make enough money to subsist, they can be, without really meaning to be, irritating.

I have been fortunate enough to visit Jamaica on mission trips with high school students about a dozen times over the past decade and a half, so I've been able to observe Jamaican life up close. I understand the pressures these shopkeepers face every day to feed their families.

In the Harbor Street Craft Market near the water's edge of Montego Bay is a shopkeeper I try to visit every time I'm on a mission trip to Jamaica. His name is Roy, and he is an encouragement to me. His life is hard as he ekes out a living by carving animals out of wood and then trying to sell them for a tiny profit in his shop.

Yet despite the disadvantages he faces, when I visit with him, he always tells me how *blessed* he is. He points happily to his open Bible on his shelf, usually mentioning that he has already been reading it that day. He also points out his well-used copy of *Our Daily Bread*.

It's hot in Roy's little stall. Often unbearably so. He dabs his brow with a dirty cloth he also uses to wipe down his carvings. It's dusty in there from the sanding he does on his carvings and from the questionable city air that settles on his sales tables. There is nothing about his shop that suggests happiness and blessing.

Nothing but Roy.

He smiles as he talks to me about the joy he has because of Jesus. It is the ready smile of the truly happy.

I always buy a carving from Roy. The last time, it was a fish I didn't need but now sits proudly in my home office as a reminder of a man who has little but Jesus yet makes it clear to his visitors that his life is blessed.

We are sometimes a little confused about what it means to be blessed—what a blessed life looks like. What the result of blessedness really is.

Some would not think of Roy as blessed, because he isn't surrounded by the trappings we often associate with God's blessing: riches, a prestigious job, a nice home with a plush lawn and a couple of late-model cars in the garage—fill in the blank with what you think a blessed person should have if he or she seems to have earned that label.

However, as we turn our attention to the Psalms life, and as we examine what this amazing book tells us about how to live, we might be in for a bit of a surprise in the blessed category.

The blessedness displayed by the writers of the psalms is not connected to cultures, to demographics, or to any of the other measuring sticks we use. It has nothing to do with having 250 channels on cable, getting a good return on your tithe, having a smoking-hot spouse, or living a trouble-free life. In fact, if we were to stick to the Psalms in our search for blessedness, we would probably laugh out loud at the commonly held idea that the person God blesses is exemplified by someone living in a Western country and basking in an upper-middle-class lifestyle.

Instead we would find that being blessed has strictly spiritual connotations and that true blessedness is available to the poorest of the poor. There is pure joy and hope in the blessed life, and we could place the label "blessed" on the heart of an elderly woman caring for her AIDS-orphaned grandchildren in a hut in Uganda just as easily as we could place it on the heart of an affluent businessman living with his wife, two kids, and a dog in Wheaton, Illinois.

Let's test this out and see what really happens to a person the writers of the psalms tell us is blessed.

• **Who is blessed?** *A sinner—a violator of God's standards—who has been forgiven by God.* "Blessed is the one whose transgressions are forgiven," David proclaims in Psalm 32:1. Here's a guy who should know. David was guilty—before God, before everyone in Israel, and before us too (because the Bible spilled the beans on him)—of two of the nastiest sins we can think of: adultery and murder. He committed sexual sin in the most blatant of ways, and then he tried to cover it up by killing his victim's husband.

Some king he was turning out to be!

But God had anointed him to fill that position. He had protected him from the wrath of his predecessor, Saul. He had allowed him to live in a big palace in Jerusalem. And this is how David says thanks: he breaks 40 percent of the Ten Commandments (he also lied, and he coveted as part of the whole Bathsheba scandal). Yet here David is, writing God-inspired words that become part of the Bible, telling us there is a way for sinners to be blessed!

It wasn't the wealth the king enjoyed that put him in the category of the blessed; it was his confession of his onerous sins before a holy God that would earn him that title.

If a wife-stealing, husband-killing, selfish king can end up being blessed, surely there's hope for the rest of us!

Sure, we'd all like to think of being blessed by God as something that will fatten our bank account or give us adoring children, but it is so much more important than that. It is the freedom, the joy, the relief, and the exhilaration of knowing that God has said to us, in effect, "I saw what you did there. I know you sinned against me. But I heard your confession, and I forgive you! I have taken your sin—your dark, horrible, ugly sin that I can't stand—and I have tossed it into the Mariana Trench." (See Google for the trench comment and Micah 7:19 for the rest.)

Miraculously, because of God's grace and forgiveness, we who are as guilty as, well, sin can walk through life free of sin's punishment (if not its consequences) and eventually enter God's presence in heaven. David's amazingly helpful testimonial on this is found in the second verse of Psalm 32: "Blessed is the one whose sin the LORD does not count against them." In the most wonderful and surprising transaction known to man, God's forgiveness pours the comfort of blessedness over the heart of the sinner who repents. Spirit-lifting forgiveness replaces the unbearable burden of guilt that weighs us down and saps us of joy. And as an added bonus, God's astounding graciousness means we sinners can become people "in whose spirit is no deceit" (v. 2).

How good is this blessedness? What does it feel like?

It's the feeling of freedom where fear once reigned. It is discovering a joy that replaces guilt. It is restoration where before there was only despair.

Think of the story of Joseph in Genesis 37–47 in the Old Testament. His brothers, who hated their father's favorite son so much that they wanted to kill him, opted instead for the less gruesome but truly disgusting "sell him into slavery" scheme. Then they washed their hands of this horrible crime against their own kin, and they sauntered on through the next several years of their lives, living a lie. It was a lie so bad, they nearly killed their father with grief.

Fast-forward a bit, and the boys end up getting deep into some hot water in Egypt. They had journeyed there to get a supply of food during a famine, but they found themselves on the wrong end of the law. They could easily have been put to death by the ruling forces for allegedly stealing from their Egyptian hosts.

Then, of all the bad luck, it turns out that the ruler who held their destiny in his hands was their very own brother—their wronged, sold, hated, and out-of-sight, out-of-mind brother. It would not have been surprising if Joseph had dispatched the whole lot of them to rot in prison for what they did to him.

Imagine the fear in the brothers' hearts as they saw their future crumble before them. Imagine how they must have regretted their long-ago decisions. Imagine how they must have been sure the book was about to be thrown at them. Their sorry scheme had come back to haunt them, and there was no way to escape punishment. "They were terrified at his presence," Genesis 45:3 tells us.

But then Joseph, gracious ruler that he was, forgave the entire bunch of them and blessed them with lands and privilege and freedom. Because godly Joseph knew about grace and knew how to bestow it on others, the brothers' fate went from probable jail and trouble to palpable joy and triumph.

That is how good the blessedness of human forgiveness feels!

That's a picture of the kind of blessedness David is trying to describe in Psalm 32:1–2 as he speaks of God's forgiveness.

It's no secret that we have all sinned. We are all in league with David and on the outs with God. But here's where it gets good. Here comes the blessing. God, in His astounding love for us, has made it abundantly simple for us to have our transgressions forgiven—to be blessed when we should be cursed.

For us, on this side of the Old Testament, Jesus's death, burial, and resurrection opened up this gift of forgiveness—the astonishingly peaceful existence of one who has had the threat of condemnation turned into the matchless blessing of the forgiven.

Who is blessed? The forgiven sinner!

• **Who is blessed?** *Someone who refuses to trust in politics, in the stock market, in the government, in his or her own talents, skills, or good looks, in science, in religion, in education, or in any other man-made provision or scheme and instead trusts in the Lord.* In another part of the Psalms, David says this: "Blessed is the one *who trusts in the LORD*, who does not look to the proud, to those who turn aside to false gods" (Psalm 40:4, emphasis added).

This is not a popular stance to take in modern society. If you were to make it known to people (not counting church folk, who we hope would be with you on this) that you were placing all of your expectations for life and happiness on capital-*G* God, many would find that idea odd.

To trust in the Lord as David described is getting more countercultural by the day. Commenting on the internet that you believe in God in a real and practical way (by saying, for example, that you really, truly trust Him) may put you in the crosshairs of trolls, but if you know what's good for you, that's okay. It's okay because the more important thing to consider is that your trust gets you the Lord's blessing. And who wouldn't trade a snide remark from a skeptic for a divine blessing from God?

Let's dig into this a little more by going to Psalm 71. This is a good place to visit when examining the blessedness of trusting God. This psalm was written by an older writer—someone who is having a Throwback Thursday moment by reflecting on the person who trusts in the Lord.

Here we see the result of what Psalm 40:4 is suggesting. We see how leaning expectantly on God's goodness instead of relying on this world's empty promises plays itself out.

Begin at Psalm 71:5–6 and marvel at what we can learn from an old man reliving his trust-life: "You have been my hope, Sovereign LORD, my confidence since my youth. From birth I have relied on you; you brought me forth from my mother's womb. I will ever praise you."

Sometimes we hear of a government attempting to give its citizens "cradle to grave" care. Whether or not that strikes a chord with you (let's not get political here), there is something comforting about someone having your back from the beginning to the end.

That is *total trust*—and that is what the writer of Psalm 71 finds to bring blessing as he relies on God throughout his life.

Year after year after year, he realizes, his life was in God's hands. As he arrives at this late stage of his life, he turns back to his Provider and says (as he has said his entire life), "I will ever praise you." As you read on in this psalm, you get to verses 9 through 13, which are typical of certain psalms, especially the ones we call "lament psalms." The writer here points out the problems brought on by those who do not support his godly stance. He talks of accusers and those who pursue him and those who want to harm him. This sounds a little twenty-first-century-ish, doesn't it, as we grow more and more alarmed with the seeming insecurity of our lives in an age of terror threats and random acts of violence.

But the writer does exactly what we need to do. He extricates himself from this "worst-case scenario" thinking by returning to his trust in God. He reimmerses himself in God's promised goodness and protection, and he lands where we all want to go: the realm of blessedness. Reading verses 17 through 24 in this chapter refocuses us on the goodness, righteousness, and comfort God provides. It reminds us why it is both wise and right to trust in Him.

> Since my youth, God, you have taught me,
>   and to this day I declare your marvelous deeds.
> Even when I am old and gray,
>   do not forsake me, my God,
> till I declare your power to the next generation,
>   your mighty acts to all who are to come.
>
> Your righteousness, God, reaches to the heavens,
>   you who have done great things.
>   Who is like you, God?
> Though you have made me see troubles,
>   many and bitter,
>   you will restore my life again;
> from the depths of the earth
>   you will again bring me up.
> You will increase my honor
>   and comfort me once more.

I will praise you with the harp
   for your faithfulness, my God;
I will sing praise to you with the lyre,
   Holy One of Israel.
My lips will shout for joy
   when I sing praise to you—
   I whom you have delivered.
My tongue will tell of your righteous acts
   all day long,
for those who wanted to harm me
   have been put to shame and confusion.
                    —Psalm 71:17–24

Think of a person you trust. I'm going to go with my wife on this one. While we may not always see eye-to-eye on everything (which I think mirrors the reality of an authentic relationship with God), I know that I can trust her to act in a way that is to our mutual benefit. I can trust that her word is true and her motive is to do the right thing.

I never have to wonder about her allegiance to our family, her concern for me, or her desire to bring good to me, our kids, and our grandchildren. It is always wise and right to trust her.

That's a picture of human trust.

And that's a little window into how the Psalm 71 psalmist saw his God-trust. Look at a couple of specifics.

1. *"You have taught me"* (v. 17).

Who does not have a favorite teacher in life? We value greatly one who can impart knowledge to us, trusting that person because he or she always points us in the direction of knowledge, which leads to wisdom. To be in the presence of one who not only conveys information but helps us learn—who teaches us—is a blessing indeed.

And no one is better at that than our God. He teaches us through His Word, through the work of His Spirit, and through the life experiences He guides us in.

In our busy, complicated world, we sometimes find it hard to sit at Jesus's feet and allow Him to teach us. We "go all Martha" on the Lord and work ourselves right out of the opportunity to learn from Him.

If that's been happening to you, perhaps it would be good to carve out some "Teacher Jesus" time, allowing yourself opportunities to examine the Gospels and listen to what He is telling you through His words and His life.

Imagine how blessed our days become when we invite Jesus to be an integral part of them.

2. *"I declare your marvelous deeds"* (v. 17).

What happens once we learn the things Jesus wants to teach us? We want to share what we've learned with others.

There are many ways we can demonstrate God's marvelous deeds to others as part of the blessed life.

We do so every time we are the one at the office who refuses to bad-talk the boss and undermine his authority.

We declare the difference God's marvelous deeds have made in our lives when we unexpectedly offer to help a neighbor with a clear need.

We remind others that our lives are about Someone much bigger than us when we respect our children's teachers, speak respectfully of leaders even if we disagree with them, and are kind to the clerks and salespeople we encounter at the stores and restaurants we frequent.

Declaring God's marvelous deeds happens when we show others that we trust God with our lives, and it happens when we demonstrate what the blessed life looks like. These examples of unrelenting belief that God is our hope and strength might even cause our friends to wonder whether they might want to try it out in their own lives.

• **Who is blessed?** *Someone who fears the Lord.* Now, it's pretty much standard-issue wisdom that no one likes to live in fear. It is not good to step into the batter's box with fear in your heart regarding the pitcher's control of his ninety-five-mile-per-hour fastball. No one wants to go to bed at night and turn out the lights fearful that someone might break into the house. There is no joy in a family when the kids and one spouse live in fear of what will happen when the other spouse comes home ready to lash out at them either physically or verbally. What employee wants to walk into a workplace afraid of being hit with abusive words or demands or even a job termination from an unscrupulous boss?

So how in the name of all that is normal and natural can a God follower be blessed if he or she *fears* the Lord? Where is the blessing in cowering before the most awesome being in the universe?

Doesn't this sound like the Force is *not* with us?

Indeed it might, if we didn't know where to turn for a great definition of what it means to fear the Lord. And that does not mean we turn to Merriam-Webster's. We turn right back to the Psalms, and we again learn from our teacher David. We listen to him as he instructs us clearly.

Look at the amazing clarity of Psalm 34:11. David says, "Come, my children, listen to me; I will teach you the fear of the LORD." Then David puts on his teacher hat and explains.

To fear the Lord: *love life and desire good days* (v. 12).

To fear the Lord: *keep your tongue away from evil; speak no lies* (v. 13).

To fear the Lord: *turn your back on evil and "spend your time in doing good"* (v. 14 TLB).

Adopting a healthy life attitude, using gracious speech, rejecting evil, and taking the time to do good things are all actions that tell the people around us that we know God, that we know His standards, and that we have enough healthy awe of our heavenly Father to honor Him with our behavior.

That's definitely a different approach from what the word *fear* would normally suggest!

Nelson's NKJV Study Bible suggests this definition for a proper fear of God: "The fear of God is an attitude of respect, a response of reverence and wonder. It is the only appropriate response to our Creator and Redeemer." Among the most respectful ways we show God we love Him is to examine His Word and find how He wants us to live, and then to live by those guidelines.

• **Who is blessed?** *The one who does not get sidetracked by the ungodly but delights in God's Word.* If there is a fundamental source of truth that informs the entire long, delightful, and challenging book of Psalms, it could very well be Psalm 1. In addition, the basis for all that has been said about the Psalms life so far is found in the two practical and informative principles that dominate the first chapter.

> Blessed is the one
>   who does not walk in step with the wicked
> or stand in the way that sinners take
>   or sit in the company of mockers,
> but whose delight is in the law of the LORD,
>   and who meditates on his law day and night.
> That person is like a tree planted by streams of water,
>   which yields its fruit in season

and whose leaf does not wither—
    whatever they do prospers.

Not so the wicked!
    They are like chaff
    that the wind blows away.
Therefore the wicked will not stand in the judgment,
    nor sinners in the assembly of the righteous.

For the LORD watches over the way of the righteous,
    but the way of the wicked leads to destruction.
                     —Psalm 1

There is a battle going on in society today. It's not a new conflict, because it has been around as far back as Cain and Abel.

But today this battle seems to have intensified as we watch the division between faith and nonfaith become clearer—and wider. In American society especially, there seems to be a concerted effort to separate people who have historic Christian faith from those who dismiss it as mythical or irrelevant or phony. We see this idea presented often when a topic regarding Christianity is brought up in a news story, for example, and the reaction is to suggest that even the idea of trusting in a God is an indication of mental imbalance.

This situation seems ironic as we consider the psalmist's view of life versus the secular view of twenty-first-century existence. The writer of Psalm 1 chose, through the guidance of the Holy Spirit, to designate the godly—those who avoid the influence of the ungodly—as blessed. As happy.

Yet being happy is also the unyielding goal of the people who this passage suggests are not to influence the godly. Let's see if I can explain what this means.

I recall talking with my now-married daughters back in the days when they were in college and working at places like department stores and grocery stores during the summer. They told me that invariably their conversations with their young coworkers would gravitate toward lifestyle—namely, partying and all that goes with it.

When my daughters would explain that as Christians, they didn't partake in some of the activities that made their coworkers' weekends exciting to them, the question came back to my girls: "So what does a Christian do for fun?"

To be happy, according to many who value their non-God-directed lives, is to engage in drunkenness, sexual activity before marriage, and other actions expressly forbidden by Scripture. Those folks listened in disbelief when they were told by their Christ-following friends that happiness comes from something as unfun as delighting in the law of the Lord.

What the ungodly think makes them happy is just what the godly are told to stay away from in order to be happy.

Therefore it is logical that this passage begins, in verse 1, by explaining three ways for the person who hopes for blessing to avoid being influenced by those who seek purpose in life outside the realm of godliness.

1. *The blessed person does not walk in the counsel of the wicked.* This has to do with whose advice one listens to. The person who wants God's blessing doesn't follow the suggestions and lifestyle recommendations of those who do not follow God's Word. Clearly, this does not mean that the blessed are to have nothing to do with the unredeemed. That is impossible for the believer and the unbeliever as they share a common existence, and the New Testament is clear that Christians are expected to have a positive influence on those who don't have faith in Jesus. But what it does mean is that

in questions that relate to godliness and Christian worldview—in setting up a philosophy or way of life—the believer who does not let the unbeliever influence him toward wrong thinking is indeed blessed.

How difficult this has become in an increasingly secular world. The ear of many a believer has been captured not by words and teachings of Scripture but by thinkers and newsmakers who possess a naturalistic worldview—one that takes a creator God out of the equation and replaces Him with random chance.

When this happens—when we take the counsel of the sweet-sounding godless thinker over the unaltered truth of Scripture—we miss out on the blessedness promised in this psalm.

2. *The blessed person does not stand in the way of the wicked.* The sinner mentioned in this passage has willfully chosen a life that is contrary to God's plan. It is not good for the follower of God to hang out with this person in a way that could lead him or her to a conclusion that runs against God's revealed Word. This means avoiding agreement with them in any matters that relate to ungodly thinking, living, or behavior.

3. *The blessed person does not sit in the seat of the scorner.* This can be a tough principle to follow for those who are forced at work or at school to listen to the teaching of one who stands opposed to God's standards. In those situations—where the believer doesn't have a choice but to hear atheism or anticreationism proclaimed—it is vital to understand the threat of negative influence.

It takes a special strength and a solid foundation in biblical thinking to sit under the teaching, for example, of a college professor who lets the class know that he or she opposes godliness and Christian principles and not be swayed toward those unbiblical views. This could be a place for accountability with a fellow believer—someone you can debrief with regarding what you are being taught. Perhaps you need someone who can guide you back on track if your thinking begins to derail.

On the other hand, when there's a choice between sitting in the seat of the scornful and avoiding that position altogether, how important it is that we run from the threat. One example of this would be the options we have regarding what kind of media we consume. Wouldn't it seem advantageous to thoughtfully avoid the possibility of being brainwashed by an ungodly philosophy in a TV program or song or movie or website?

God's blessing is a wonderful thing, but it sometimes requires us to make hard decisions about who or what influences us.

• **Who is blessed?** *The one who delights in God's law and meditates on it.*

The lunch break at work is a thirty-minute oasis from the daily grind. For that half hour, employees get to do what they really love doing—and for most of them, that includes eating. But some take delight in doing other things as well. Perhaps they love playing board games, so they get a few friends together for a quick competition. Others love to soak up the sun, so they go outside to catch rays. Others delight in cracking open the web and catching up with Facebook happenings. I enjoy going online to read the news of the day from my favorite island nation, Jamaica.

We do what brings us delight, even if it is for just 1,800 seconds.

That's why I'm impressed with Ted. Every day when I see him during lunchtime at work, he is munching a sandwich and reading the Bible. Ted clearly delights in opening God's Word and seeing what nuggets he can mine in his short break period.

To me, Ted exemplifies delighting in God's Word. He is not reading it because he has to or to prepare a lesson or even write a book. He is poring over it while pouring his second cup of coffee because he *wants* to. Ted is blessed!

When we find it delightful to open up our copies of Scripture and meditate on its grand teachings, God smiles on us. He is happy with us. We are blessed.

Twice blessed, actually. Blessed because of God's approval and blessed because of God's teachings and His story as spelled out in the Bible's thirty-one thousand verses.

The book of Psalms is a doorway to the blessed life. It opens with a call for us to use God's Word—not people—as our guide. It later reminds us of the necessity of seeking forgiveness of our sins. It challenges us to have a righteous and right fear of the Lord. And it explains the importance of trusting nothing in life as much as we trust our God.

Those are the elements that lead to true happiness—true blessedness before God as we exist in a world that doesn't think too highly of either our faith or our heavenly Father. As we work our way through what can be called the Psalms life, let's start there. Let's incorporate these valuable principles into our everyday existence and then bask in the blessedness God offers.

T w o

The Examined Life

The most famous quote on self-reflection came from the quill of Plato, who lived and philosophized in Athens, Greece, as the Old Testament era was coming to a close (Plato died around 347 BC). This great student of Socrates and teacher of Aristotle (how's that for a resume?) quoted Socrates, who said, "The unexamined life is not worth living."

Centuries later, Kurt Vonnegut, who wrote books such as *Slaughterhouse-Five*, mused, "Plato says that the unexamined life is not worth living. But what if the examined life turns out to be a clunker as well?"

Nobody wants life to be a clunker, and indeed some people who are introspective may end up with life that is more 1985 Yugo and less brand-new Lexus. This means we must gain a clear understanding of what it means to examine our lives—to take a good, long look inside to see what, if anything, we need to do to make life work better as we seek to glorify God with the days He has given us. Clearly, we can find ourselves mired in complacency and bogged down in difficulties if we don't think about where our lives are going. Humans are not made to run rampant through life without moments of self-evaluation.

Yes, the examined life may end up being a bit of a clunker— since life is more than introspection—but the unexamined life has no hope of becoming a shiny classic for the world to admire.

Buried at the end of one of the most remarkable psalms on record is David's personal invitation to the examined life. In Psalm 139:23–24, the most prolific psalm writer said this: "Search me, God, and know my heart; test me and know my anxious thoughts. See if there is any offensive way in me." Here, at the end of a psalm that tells us there is nothing hidden from God's view (vv. 1–4), David asks God in for a look around. He opens his heart to the Lord so God can find and extract anything in David's life that is offensive.

What makes David's statement so powerful to us is his past. Of anyone we see in the pages of Scripture, David would be voted Least Likely to Want to Let God Examine His Life. He represents all of us who have thought we could run away from God without getting caught or figured we could contrive some scheme in the darkness that God couldn't see in His light. As was mentioned in chapter 1, David smashed through the barriers of the Ten Commandments on his way to temporary pleasure.

So why would he want God to search him and know his heart? Perhaps it is because at this point in his life, David has realized that the examined life far outshines the hidden life of concealed sin. Perhaps it is because Psalm 51 is behind him—a psalm that draws the line in David's life between the grinding sorrow of sin and the grand sweetness of forgiveness.

Before Psalm 51, David lived with the words of his court prophet Nathan hanging over him like a noxious cloud: "You are the man!

. . . Why did you despise the word of the LORD by doing what is evil in his eyes?" (2 Samuel 12:7, 9). And then how could David escape what in his thinking really should have been the fatal blow to his relationship with God: "You struck down Uriah the Hittite with the sword and took his wife to be your own. . . . Now, therefore, the sword will never depart from your house" (vv. 9–10).

If that explains for us the intense disappointment in himself David must have felt because of his sin against God and his fellow man, we might also feel some of the relief the king experienced later after he discovered that he could be forgiven through God's mercy. This forgiveness is the result of and ultimate reward for the self-examination of Psalm 51.

Let's take a look at this chapter that turned things around for David—a chapter that can give us hope in the middle of the dark night of sin and give us joy when all around is the crushing sound of defeat and sadness over our transgressions.

For David, and for us, Psalm 51 is the journey that takes us to the examined life. Let's look at the route David takes and see how we can relate to it as we seek to live this part of the Psalms life.

Step 1: David Casts Himself on God's Mercy (vv. 1–2)

A recent court case that I watched shows us a lot about the danger of casting yourself on someone else's mercy, unless you trust that person. A man who had been convicted of a serious crime had an opportunity to ask a judge to reduce his sentence. Apparently, the state sentencing guidelines used by the judge in the original case were later struck down by a higher court. Therefore the man could ask for a reduction in the time he would have to serve in prison. However, if he opened the case again, he'd risk the possibility that the opposite would happen. The judge could *increase* the sentence, keeping him in prison longer.

The problem was, the man did not trust that the judge would rule in his favor.

For that reason, it was hard for him to throw himself on the judge's mercy, so he didn't seek resentencing.

That is not the way things are with God. We can have 100 percent trust in Him. We can reveal to Him our sin in all of its ugliness, knowing that the Judge of all the world will do what is right (Genesis 18:25). He has explained to us in clear terms what happens when we repent. He is not some mysterious judge who may hold a grudge against us, attempt to make a name for himself, or try to make an example of us! He has promised us over and over that forgiveness is ours in exchange for our heartfelt and honest confession.

Notice the words David used when he hurled himself on the mercy of God: "according to your unfailing love; according to your great compassion" (Psalm 51:1). When we examine our lives and discover that we have somehow offended God, we can do nothing better than to speak to Him about our sin, clearly confess it, and ask forgiveness. Take a look at the positive result of that action: the unbreakable promise of God's unfailing love, and the guarantee of His incomparable compassion.

When we access God's mercy, we don't cast ourselves into an abyss of uncertainty, wondering what God is going to do to us. We find in Him a comforting, forgiving presence—and a release to the freedom that comes from being set loose from sin's grip. That's the result of the washing away that verse 2 so brightly offers.

Step 2: David Recognizes Who He Has Sinned Against (vv. 3–4)

Imagine a situation in which a teenage son takes a pathway toward rebellion. Although his parents have done the best they can to instill in him good values such as honesty and integrity, he decides one day to shoplift a bunch of stuff from the local Walmart.

Everyone is aghast when the phone call comes from the police, announcing that the youngster has been arrested. There is plenty of hurt to go around as the family deals with this embarrassing situation. The parents, naturally, feel the greatest pain.

Months later a new development occurs. The parents go to a special savings box they have hidden in their house, planning to pull out some cash. But it is empty. They know immediately what happened. Their son has stolen hundreds of dollars from them.

When he stole from Walmart, the parents were deeply hurt. But when he stole from them directly, they were devastated.

Both deeds were wrong, but it crushed Mom and Dad to discover that their son would steal from those he knew and loved.

One must wonder if it's a little like that with God. When we, as God's children, offend Him by disobeying His clear standards in Scripture—when we sin, as David said, "against you, you only" (v. 4)—how much it must hurt our heavenly Father!

David recognized that pain and in his confession acknowledged it. Further, he said that he had "done what is evil in [God's] sight" (v. 4), affirming that God's words were accurate regarding right and wrong. And David also stated that God's judgment on his life—whatever that judgment might be—would be justified.

An awareness of David's confession is a major challenge for us. It condemns us when we try to hide our sin from God or try to talk ourselves out of our guilt. It pinpoints the fallacy of thinking there is such a thing as a little sin, because each transgression is a direct and blatant offense against our crucified Savior. And it nullifies any inkling that our sin is no big deal and doesn't need to be dealt with.

The need for an examined life can easily be ignored as we live on this side of Calvary. We sometimes bask in the "positional sanctification" afforded us through our salvation, knowing that our sins have been forgiven and our heavenly destination is assured because we have put our faith in Jesus's finished work on the cross. But we forget the reality that sin can still have negative effects on us.

If we allow sin to go unexamined and unaddressed, two serious results may cast a pall over our lives. First, sin has consequences, and even if our sins are forgiven through salvation and through a 1 John 1:9 confession, the negative effects can linger.

That teenager in our story may have trusted Jesus as his Savior earlier in his life but was now rebelling against God and family. Let's say he eventually allowed the Holy Spirit to convict him of his bad actions and lead him to realize that he was on the wrong road and needed to repent of his stealing. He confessed his sin to the Lord and received the full measure of forgiveness.

His position in the kingdom of God, however, would not negate any legal ramifications of his wrongdoing.

Sure, God could intervene and miraculously allow the teen to miss out on the normal punishment of the legal system, but generally speaking, his sin would have consequences.

Second, sin robs us of the most important relationship we can have—fellowship with our Father in heaven. Unconfessed sin harms our connection to the One who knows us, cares for us, watches over us, and desires to hear from us. That leaves us with a horrible void in our lives.

If we are serious about our efforts to live the examined life, we will recognize the seriousness of our sin, because it is against God himself. We will rush to confess it and reestablish a connection with the One whose love is immeasurable.

Step 3: David Recognizes His DNA (vv. 5–6)

True, this seems a bit anachronistic. David, though king of the land and in charge of all the smartest people under his rulership, was not aware of DNA. But he did understand the essence of man's common heritage: he, like everyone else born on this planet, was sinful at birth.

This can remind us that the examined life is for everyone.

As I was writing this book, our daughter Julie delivered her third child—the third girl for her and her husband, Ewing. Even before she was born, they gave her the name Mollie. She will grow up to be cute, smart, and a fun combination of her older siblings, Katie and Maggie.

She has two parents who will take wonderful care of her and teach her godly things her whole life. She'll go to Sunday school and Awana, and she'll learn all the Bible stories.

She'll sing "Jesus Loves Me" and "This Little Light of Mine," and she'll probably like TobyMac as much as her sisters do.

And she'll be a sinner.

Just like that nasty brother named Cain in the book of Genesis—the one who killed his own sibling—and all of the billions of babies born since him.

Nearly seven and a half billion people roam this earth, and every last one of them was sinful at birth. Cute, huggable, ready to have their image posted on Facebook for all to marvel at, but sinners nonetheless.

It's our shared DNA that makes living the examined life essential. If we do not take stock of our hearts on a regular basis, the sin that got passed down to us through Adam and Eve will eventually be our undoing.

Without examining our lives and recognizing the damage caused by this universal problem of sin, we will be pulled down by our guilt. Notice how David shows the value of being aware of our sin and then taking it to God for forgiveness: "I acknowledged my sin to you and did not cover up my iniquity" (Psalm 32:5). We read a lot about cover-ups by politicians and other public figures.

These folks get caught, and then the backpedaling begins. Often they go to great lengths to avoid being convicted of their wrong-doing. And if they get away with it long enough that people stop paying attention, they think they'll never have to say they're sorry.

That is a heavy burden to bear. In Psalm 38:18, David says what we all know to be true: "I am troubled by my sin." None of us is strong enough to carry around the weight of unforgiven sin without some hope of relief. That's why, after our self-examination reveals our offense, we need to say with David, "I will confess my transgressions to the LORD" (Psalm 32:5). When we do, we can also echo David in saying, "You forgave the guilt of my sin" (v. 5).

So, recognizing that we are born to sin, we realize that our route to joy in the examined life is to admit our guilt and find the freedom of forgiveness.

Step 4: David Recognizes That Regeneration Is from God (vv. 7–10)

Sin is deadly.

When the bill comes due for our sin, the bottom line has the word *death* written on it. James penned these harrowing words: "After desire has conceived, it gives birth to sin; and sin, when it is full-grown, gives birth to death" (James 1:15). Sin leads to death.

We are all therefore "dead in [our] transgressions and sins" (Ephesians 2:1). And we will all stay that way unless something drastically changes.

Psalm 51:7–10 details for us what that change looks like and what rewards come to us when we seek God's remedy for deadly sin.

"Cleanse me . . . wash me" (v. 7). Filthy from his sin and ready to seek a remedy, David discovers that he needs to be cleansed—he needs to be washed. The example he gives is that of a leper being cleansed with hyssop. Then he uses a different image, one we are

more familiar with: to be washed whiter than snow. Both images call for great celebration. To be scrubbed clean of the sin that threatens to send us to a godless eternity is reason to plan a party.

"Let me hear joy and gladness" (v. 8). A good picture of the party that should follow the washing away of sin is found in Isaiah 35. There we see ransomed saints entering Zion "with singing; everlasting joy will crown their heads. Gladness and joy will overtake them" (v. 10).

The once dead are made alive through God's cleansing, and unrestrained joy accompanies them as they enter God's presence. This grand result of a life examined and then presented to God to be fixed by His grace can remind us of both the joy of salvation and the freedom of sins forgiven.

"Hide your face from my sins . . . blot out all my iniquity" (v. 9). When you remember the awfulness of David's sin, you can easily recognize the value of this request. It bookends this portion of David's confession (see v. 1) and again reminds us of the importance of God's full forgiveness.

Step 5: David Enjoys Renewal (vv. 10–12)

A few years ago, I got to observe an amazing example of love and compassion while in Jamaica on one of those mission trips mentioned earlier. On several occasions, we visited a home for handicapped children and young adults near Montego Bay. As a leader of this group, I was always touched by the care and love our kids gave the residents.

One of the children we saw year after year was Donald, a young teen who had what appeared to be cerebral palsy. He hardly moved, and his muscles seemed to have atrophied for lack of use. Some of our students would feed him, for he couldn't feed himself. He couldn't talk, but he did have a big smile for his caregivers.

One year when we were in Jamaica, we heard news that seemed too good to be true. An American couple had adopted Donald, and they were going to come to get him while we were there.

Indeed it happened, and after Donald's new parents picked him up, they came to the place where we were staying. Our students, a choir, sang to him and his parents. There were smiles and tears all around.

Today Donald is something of a media superstar. I have seen him and his parents on social media, and they have been featured on TV news programs. Donald and his dad do marathons, with Dad pushing the wheelchair and Donald smiling and laughing. It is amazing to see his transformation over the years. He has even learned how to walk a little bit!

Renewal! While the folks who cared for Donald in Jamaica did everything they could for him, they were limited by logistics and money and lack of personnel. Now he has a mom and dad who have poured their lives into him, and he has an amazing new life.

Renewal! That's what David receives. And the transformation is dramatic.

In verse 10, he is asking God to give him a new heart—a heart chasing not after sin and deceit but after God. David asks to be renewed with a steadfast spirit.

And this: "Restore to me the joy of your salvation" (v. 12).

Isn't that what we all need? Isn't that the goal of our hearts every time we recognize that we have stepped away from God's loving presence and ventured out on our own sinful path? Don't we recall the joy of sins forgiven and the freshness of renewed relationship and want to run back into our Father's arms?

David did that, and we can too.

Renewal. It's there for us every time we need it. Enjoy it by examining your life and asking God to "blot out [your] transgressions" (v. 1).

Step 6: David Tells Others (vv. 13–15)

Sometimes it's the people who were the deepest in sin who are the best at extracting sinners from a similar life. Chuck Colson, who it was said would run over his own grandmother to help his political agenda and cronies, led an entire generation to understand what it means to be born again. David Wilkerson was a gang member with no concern for others until he turned to Jesus and began to lead thousands to a transformed life of faith in Christ.

And David seems to be heading that way too. The disgraced king, having received God's grace, tells us in Psalm 51 what his next step will be.

"I will teach transgressors your ways, so that sinners will turn back to you" (v. 13). And how is he going to do this? "Open my lips, Lord, and my mouth will declare your praise" (v. 15).

No, we don't have to be a redeemed political hatchet man, a rescued gang member, or a restored abuser and murderer to do what David is describing, but the fact that these three can proclaim God's Word should challenge us to do the same.

In living the examined life, we also need to peer into our world and see if there are those to whom we can, as David did, declare God's praise.

Plato was partially right. He had the right idea about living the examined life, but he left out the details about how we should do so. We learn that from another great man of history, David, and we go away equipped to keep our hearts close to God while thinking of ways to bring others to Him. Those are the two main goals of the examined life.

T h r e e

The Guided Life

She was beautiful. She was athletic. She sought to make other people happy. She loved Jesus.

But on June 6, 2002, at the age of seventeen—on the last day of her junior year of high school—our daughter Melissa Ruth Branon was suddenly and tragically taken from Sue and me and our other three children in a car accident.

She left the house that morning to take her last exams for the school year, and then it was off to the beach to enjoy the fun of being with her friends from the Christian school she attended. She had parked her little white Chevy Beretta at school that morning, planning to get a ride back to school in the evening to pick it up and then come on home.

She never made it back to her car, which her friends decorated in her memory the next day as it sat alone and forlorn in the school parking lot.

It has been more than fifteen years since we last enjoyed Melissa's presence in our family, yet as I wrote those words, I sobbed.

I. Can. Not. Believe. She. Is. Gone.

Look, I know I am not alone in this sadness. I know losing a child is not unique, and I realize I do not have a corner on the sorrows of life. Perhaps you could tell me bitter stories of how life has taken a horrible turn for you and tossed you to the side of the road, battered and bruised.

So I don't tell you about Melissa because I need any more sympathy, nor do I want anybody's pity. I tell you our story because of what I have learned through our tearful journey. What we've learned about our God. What we've discovered about His Word.

But mostly to tell you what we have found to be true about God's guidance.

In living the Psalms life, as has already been noted, two of our top priorities are to live the blessed life, as spelled out in passages like Psalm 1, and to live the examined life, as David showed us in Psalm 51. Now it is time to take a close look at what the great book of poetry and wisdom tells us about letting God guide us through our day-to-day existence. Once we have understood how to seek true happiness and how to allow God to extricate us from the penalty and isolation of sin, we move on to asking for His guidance through the ups and downs of life. And one of the best places to start in seeking God's direction is Psalm 139.

> You have searched me, LORD,
>   and you know me.
> You know when I sit and when I rise;
>   you perceive my thoughts from afar.
> You discern my going out and my lying down;
>   you are familiar with all my ways.
> Before a word is on my tongue
>   you, LORD, know it completely.

You hem me in behind and before,
　　and you lay your hand upon me.
Such knowledge is too wonderful for me,
　　too lofty for me to attain.
Where can I go from your Spirit?
　　Where can I flee from your presence?
If I go up to the heavens, you are there;
　　if I make my bed in the depths, you are there.
If I rise on the wings of the dawn,
　　if I settle on the far side of the sea,
even there your hand will guide me,
　　your right hand will hold me fast.
If I say, "Surely the darkness will hide me
　　and the light become night around me,"
even the darkness will not be dark to you;
　　the night will shine like the day,
　　for darkness is as light to you.
For you created my inmost being;
　　　you knit me together in my mother's womb.
I praise you because I am fearfully and wonderfully made;
　　your works are wonderful,
　　I know that full well.
My frame was not hidden from you
　　when I was made in the secret place,
　　when I was woven together in the depths of the earth.
Your eyes saw my unformed body;
　　all the days ordained for me were written in your book
　　before one of them came to be.
How precious to me are your thoughts, God!
　　How vast is the sum of them!
Were I to count them,

they would outnumber the grains of sand—
    when I awake, I am still with you.
If only you, God, would slay the wicked!
    Away from me, you who are bloodthirsty!
They speak of you with evil intent;
    your adversaries misuse your name.
Do I not hate those who hate you, LORD,
    and abhor those who are in rebellion against you?
I have nothing but hatred for them;
    I count them my enemies.
Search me, God, and know my heart;
    test me and know my anxious thoughts.
See if there is any offensive way in me,
    and lead me in the way everlasting.

—Psalm 139

Did you ever have someone come to your church to preach as a visiting speaker, and as he gave his sermon, he hit all the wrong notes? Or it could have been a substitute teacher in school who simply did not have the pulse of the classroom.

Or maybe this, if you are a sports fan like me: You tune in to a national broadcast of your favorite team's game, and you wince every time these announcers—who are unfamiliar with your team—start talking about the team you know better than they do. "The manager likes to bunt in this situation," one of them intones, and you know very well that your skipper hasn't had a batter lay one down for two weeks.

In all of those situations—the bewildered preacher who unwittingly jokes about something the church has just struggled through, the substitute who gets all the classroom rules wrong, or the misinformed baseball guys—someone who does not know enough about the situation gets caught up in a major fail. We hate it when that happens.

Now take a look at Psalm 139:1–4. Look at all the ways God reminds us how much He knows about us—that there can never be a time when He comes into our lives without being armed with all the facts. When it comes to you and me, God is never uninformed or left in the dark.

- He has searched us (v. 1).
- He knows when we move around the room (v. 2).
- He knows what we are thinking (v. 2)!
- He knows when we head out for work and when we come home for a nice nap (v. 3).
- He even knows what we are going to say before we can get the words out (v. 4). (That's something most of us can't even do as we talk.)

God is never in the bind of the ill-informed preacher, the ill-prepared substitute teacher, or the ill-equipped baseball announcer. Our heavenly Father knows us better than we know ourselves. We never have to worry that He will lead us incorrectly because He can't quite figure out what is best for us. He never bobbles a decision or leads us astray or miscalculates our needs.

So as we begin to look at the value of the guided life under God's direction, we have this comfort and this confidence: He is a guide whose intimate knowledge of us is essential to the way He influences us toward right actions. He knows our skill level. He knows our interests. He knows our propensities and our dislikes. He knows what is hard for us and what is easy for us. He knows who we depend on for help. And He always, always knows what will bring himself the most glory while allowing us to represent Him in the best possible way.

But as we venture deeper into Psalm 139, we discover another dimension of God's guidance. This goes beyond how His thorough knowledge of us gives us confidence to move on in the day-to-day dealings of life. This has to do with a bigger-picture view of God. This has to do with our very being—our creation as a human and then our total existence on earth.

Verses 13 and 14 take a page from science to demonstrate God's hand in our conception and development: "You created my inmost being; you knit me together in my mother's womb" (v. 13).

Our very existence is something that involved God's creative hand. What an amazing thought! God takes credit for being your Creator, my Creator. He takes credit for your existence!

Think of the astounding implications that stem from having the great God of the universe intricately involved in the simple fact of our presence on this earth. This means that we are in His care in the most intimate way. As a product of His creative skills, we are forever connected to Him as His workmanship. And, as other Scripture tells us, we share something no other created being shares: God's image.

Think of what this means. God deeply loves us as carriers of His image. He wants the best for us. He is eager to provide us guidance and help for life through the power of the Holy Spirit. Go back to one of the key verses we looked at in Psalm 51 when we took a look at the examined life. In verse 11, we read David's plea to God: "Do not . . . take your Holy Spirit from me." David realized that if he was, through God's mercies, to return to the Father's fellowship and regain the Lord's power in his life, he needed the presence of God's Spirit. While we do need to maintain our fellowship with God, as David strove to do in Psalm 51, those of us who have been born into God's family through faith in Jesus know that the Holy Spirit will never be cast away from us.

And that means we have the assurance of God's constant guidance. The One who created us and cares for us has equipped us with the Holy Spirit as a guidance system. The Spirit guides us into a clearer understanding of the Bible. He guides us away from temptation when it threatens to lead us to sin. He guides us to recall God's truth as we discuss it with others (John 14:26). He guides us by quietly directing us in our daily decisions.

As we contemplate the grand truth of God's loving guidance in our lives, we also recognize that it is possible for the difficult realities of our existence to get in the way. I contemplate that in relation to losing Melissa. Sue and I felt that we were indeed following God's Holy Spirit guidance in raising our children. For instance, we felt strongly that God wanted Melissa to be educated at a Christian school.

But on that horrible June day, it did her no good (humanly speaking) to be with her friends from that school and to be enjoying her last day of school with them. They were not doing anything wrong; that is not the point.

However, we could look at it like this: Had she gone to a different school and had different friends, she would not have been at that intersection at the wrong time. She would not have lost her life had her circumstances, which we caused in one sense by our schooling decision, been different.

And there is this consideration: Can this be a loving and all-wise guidance behind the scenes, orchestrating things, if in the end our loving Christian family is shattered by an out-of-the-blue phone call on a beautiful June evening? Where is the love for us when it is our daughter who doesn't come home that night, while everyone else made it safely to their front door? When it is our family that has to pack up her roomful of cherished belongings, never to be used again? When it is our future that will forever be troubled by the empty chair?

How could God have given us this wonderful yet flawed teenager to love and cherish, and let us pour our lives into her, just to snatch her away from us when she is on the cusp of adulthood? Just when she is nearly prepared to make her mark for Jesus on the world? Just when all our hopes and dreams for her are being realized? What kind of guidance is that?

We continue to crawl through the verses of Psalm 139—the psalm that tells us God created Melissa in a special way and fashioned her to be a fearfully and wonderfully made bearer of His image—and we discover a heart-pounding truth that encapsulates God's guidance in our lives, in Melissa's life.

It's a truth that helps Sue and me when we fret over any choices we made that ended up putting Melissa in what we could easily call the wrong place at the wrong time. And it is a truth that helps me to realize that although the person Melissa was riding with made a driving error that night, I cannot place the blame for her death at that person's feet. This truth allows me to act graciously toward that person when my human nature might choose a different approach.

This is not a truth that makes everything okay, nor does it take away the pain. It doesn't stop our tears or our sighs. But it does give us a universal perspective on life that helps us deal with reality, while reminding us that we are not in control.

Psalm 139:16 says this: "All the days ordained for me were written in your book before one of them came to be."

There is no room for happenstance in this verse.

There is room only for God's sovereignty. For God's total knowledge of our existence (see vv. 1–4). For a detailed plan for life—a life limited on this side of heaven by our "days ordained" but unlimited on the other side by timelessness. In other words, my abject sorrow in losing my little girl in what we think was an untimely accident can be tempered by the reality that God gave her to us for the exact and perfect period of time He designed for her. His guidance of us and our guidance of her were not at odds.

Sometimes when tragedy crashes into our lives and steals what is most important to us, we might conclude that we no longer want to worship and honor a God who doesn't stop things like this. We can suddenly decide that all of God's eternal schedule—His plan of redemption through Jesus—is flawed and must be rejected. In other words, if it doesn't work out my way, it simply doesn't work.

"Guide all you want, God, but check with me first." That's the reality of our thinking if we decide to throw out the grand scheme of God's plan because we think the trajectory of our lives has gone off course.

But our tragedy is not an indication that God's plan or His guidance is spinning out of control. It is instead a reminder to look at God's big picture, at what has been called the metanarrative of Scripture. While God's guidance certainly extends to us in the days that He has ordained for us, it is also at work in the big plan of creation-fall-redemption that we see moving throughout Scripture.

Each of us, as believers in Jesus Christ, has a role in that grand plan. That is our primary reason for existence—to make disciples of others through Holy Spirit guidance. Some are called to have a dynamic influence on hundreds of thousands of people before the final pages of their book are written; think Billy Graham. Some are called to sparkle brightly for a short time through an influence on a small group of people; think Melissa. And some of the rest of us are left behind to extend the influence of one such as Melissa so others can be comforted, guided, encouraged, and lifted up; think our family, friends, and people who read my writings in *Our Daily Bread* and my books.

God's guidance of each of us believers is centered on one thing: how can we influence those around us for Jesus Christ?

Think for a moment about Ephesians 2:10. This is an amazing and challenging verse that reminds us of the Psalm 139 truths of God's total knowledge of us and His sovereignty in our lives. Paul said, "We are God's handiwork, created in Christ Jesus to do good works, *which God prepared in advance for us to do*" (emphasis added). Remember what Psalm 139:4 says: "Before a word is on my tongue you know it completely"? This is something like that. Before we go to the soup kitchen to feed the hungry, God has preordained that task for us to fulfill. Before we stop by a coworker's office and say, "Rough day? Can we go out for lunch?" God knows that person needs our Christlike compassion.

Does God guide us? Indeed He does.

He knows us, and He has a plan for what He wants us to do.

Let's take a closer look at the nuances of God's guidance as presented in the Psalms.

For instance, there's a prayer in Psalm 25 that outlines for us the path to true guidance.

As David cries out to God in this psalm, he mentions that he has enemies and that he does not want those enemies to triumph over him (v. 2). He suggests that putting his hope in God will ensure that the enemies will end up being put to shame (v. 3). After that, he asks for guidance: "Show me your ways, LORD, teach me your paths. Guide me in your truth and teach me" (vv. 4–5).

Frank Sinatra, an icon from another era, sang, "I did it my way." More recently, Bon Jovi created a version of that philosophy with "It's My Life." The ideas of these two very different musical talents contrast greatly with David's prayer. The heart's desire of those two songsters is this: I want my ways, my paths, and my truth to prevail. I am in charge of my own destiny, and my success depends on the one and only *me*!

David, however, asks for guidance from a source outside himself. He found out, as we've already discussed, that following a do-it-yourself plan can lead straight into serious sin.

So David requests that God's ways, God's paths, and God's truth be his guides.

If we want to live the guided life, we have to agree with David here and be willing to turn over control of our lives to God. We should discover what God's ways might be, by examining His Word to learn its principles. We should discover what God's paths for us are—how we walk through this life on the level, straight routes suggested to us by Psalm 27:11 and Psalm 143:8. And we should discover God's truth—His doctrine, if you will—so we can live by it.

The guided life's theme verse, then, should be Psalm 119:105: "Your word is a lamp for my feet, a light on my path."

Let's look at each of David's three requests for guidance in Psalm 25.

• *God's ways.* Righteousness is one of God's most important ways to live. Psalm 5:8 says, "Lead me, LORD, in your righteousness . . . make your way straight before me." God honors this search for doing what is right: "The LORD has dealt with me according to my righteousness; according to the cleanness of my hands he has rewarded me" (18:20). Living the guided life helps us avoid the difficulties we might otherwise get ourselves into, as we focus on God and not on ourselves.

• *God's paths.* A nephew of mine recently told me of something that happened on a mission trip to Peru. In the city where he was working, there was a large market that extended for many blocks. He decided to explore it on his own, but before he left, he tried to recall what side street he had walked down to get there, so he could return to where he was staying. However, the market stretched much farther than he imagined it would. When he finished his excursion, he turned around to go back. However, he noticed that there were side streets by the dozens, and he could no longer recognize which was his. In effect, he was lost because he didn't know which path to take.

He was eventually able to find the right one, but he was quite frightened for a while, fearful of being lost in a city where he did not know the language.

As we journey through the marketplace of life, it can grow increasingly difficult to know which path to take. There are so many choices. There are so many decisions about how to live, how to think, who we can trust, and what direction our lives should take. There are many possible paths, and we can get really confused.

That's why we would agree with David's prayer: "Teach me *your* paths" (Psalm 25:4, emphasis added). As we venture out into the world, we need God's help to know which way to turn. Without Him as our pathway guide, we can easily wander around in fear and near panic, like my nephew did.

As we seek God's paths, we can look at the psalms and proverbs in the Bible to find out more about how God's guidance helps us. Psalm 73:24 says, "You guide me with your counsel." This counsel, or advice, this explanation of purpose that comes from God, is eternally good (Psalm 33:11), it accompanies wisdom (Proverbs 8:14; 12:15), and it stands alone among man's options for finding the right way to live (Proverbs 19:21).

You know the various paths people take in life, and usually these paths reflect how well they listen to God's counsel. The young person who decides to turn his back on the church and on faith will take paths that often he learns to regret. The parent who takes paths that don't reflect godly teaching and concern for the family will reap windstorms of trouble in future years.

Our paths lead someplace, and unless we allow God to guide those paths with His omniscience and His love, how can we expect to keep our lives going in the right direction?

• *God's truth.* As we look at Psalm 25 one more time, we notice that David speaks of something that has fallen on hard times in recent years: truth. The guided life is controlled by truth—namely, God's truth. That is, the life of the faithful believer—the one who wants to live in the light of God's sovereignty and guidance—will be in every possible way managed by God's truth. "Guide me in your truth," says David (v. 5).

Acting on God's truth is a powerful way to live the guided life. It provides us with security, a blanket of protection. At the end of Psalm 139, David says, "Lead me in the way everlasting" (v. 24). God's truth is eternal; it is the everlasting revelation that will accompany us both now and forever. This way represents a path that walks us past the dangers of temptation and the threats of our enemy.

The guided life sounds wonderful, doesn't it? Let's experience it by living in the comfort of God's sovereignty and in the protection of God's direction through following His ways, His paths, and His truth.

Four

The Worshiping Life

I'm guessing here, but the best I can figure, I've watched or listened to at least some part of about 6,000 baseball games. Between my growing-up love for the Cincinnati Reds and my post-college affection for the Detroit Tigers (via my transplant to Michigan), I have observed just about anything that can happen on the diamond. No wonder my wife often observes that when I make a comment about the game, the announcers repeat what I just said.

After all those games, I keep watching. I follow the schedule every day to know when the Tigers are going to be on TV, so I can keep an eye on them. After all those thousands and thousands of innings, I am still interested in the game and all of its nuances. I still cheer on my team!

I'm guessing again, but the best I can figure, I have gone to church about 4,500 times in my life. Like watching baseball, this habit started when I was young, and it has continued to be a part of my life week after week after week.

I've heard all the songs. I've endured all the announcements. I've put thousands of dollars on the plate. I've heard messages from every book in the Bible, many times over. And after all of those thousands of hours in the pew (chairs now), I am still interested. I still love going. I still enjoy gathering with other believers to see what God is going to teach us and how He is going to be worshiped.

And I know that millions of other believers are with me on this. We love to go into the house of the Lord to worship God—to bring glory and honor to Him with our words and actions.

As we do, we continue on in the heart of the worship pattern that is presented in such fascinating ways in the book of Psalms. Clearly, the Psalms life is the worshiping life.

In fact, there is an entire section of the Psalms that relates to the worship of the people of Israel. From that section (called the Songs of Ascent), and from other passages in the book, we can learn some valuable lessons about worship.

Before we visit the people of Israel as they march along to the tune of favorite worship songs of the day, let's visit a call-to-worship passage in the Psalms that can encourage us to lift our hearts and voices in praise. It's Psalm 95, about which Charles Haddon Spurgeon, the great nineteenth-century British preacher, said, "It has about it a ring like that of the church bells."

What draws you to worship the Lord?

Our worship is mostly contained in our church building, where we gather to sing out our praises to the glory of God. At other times, we voice our praises as we listen to a radio station that plays God-honoring music while we travel in the car. Or we may quietly praise God, without the benefit of music, at numerous times throughout the day. Observing creation, reading the Bible, enjoying the exuberance of children, basking in the warmth of a positive relationship—these can all be times when we worship God for what He has provided for us.

But what is it that leads us to dedicate our hearts to worship?

In my years of teaching and studying British literature, I grew to appreciate the poetic collections of William Wordsworth. But I think the line I most appreciate from this remarkable nineteenth-century poet from the Lake District of England comes not from his poetry but from Wordsworth's study of poetics— how poetry works.

In attempting to convey what poetry is, Wordsworth described it as "the spontaneous overflow of powerful feelings . . . recollected in tranquility." Doesn't that sound a lot like worship? Our hearts contemplate who God is, in our quiet moments of reflection, and as a result of our contemplation the words and the tunes that come from our mouths represent a powerful overflow of our loving thoughts toward our Lord.

In Psalm 95, we can see that powerful overflow; we can sense those feelings as the singers of this passage commemorate the rebuilding of the temple in Jerusalem. Their hearts burst forth in praise for what God has done, praise that comes from an overflow of powerful feelings of gratitude.

They sing for joy, they "shout aloud to the Rock of our salvation," and they offer thanksgiving while extoling the Lord with music and song (vv. 1–2).

This psalm lifts our hearts in praise and reminds us again why we value the worshiping life. It reminds us of God's greatness (v. 3). It refreshes our understanding of God's creative power (vv. 4–5). And it calls us again to worship (vv. 6–7), reminding us that God is greater than we are, yet He cares for us.

It affirms once more that the worshiping life is such an important component of living the Psalms life.

Worship Details

I've mentioned the thousands of times I have worshiped the Lord in a church service. Since I used such big numbers to describe both my Major League Baseball attention and my church attendance, you can surmise that both started many decades ago.

That leads me to an interesting point about what we normally call worship these days—corporate worship inside a church building. What we called worship back in the days of Eisenhower and Kennedy sometimes bears little resemblance to the worship we enjoy now. In the communities I grew up in, anything faster than "Just As I Am" was unheard of—and unheard—in church. There were no drums, guitars, or praise teams. A robed choir or a soloist sang "special" music—another slow and old song (I am not complaining; I've loved worship through all of its stages during my life).

It's probably not like that in your church today (if I'm wrong, my bad on this point), but this is not about the "right" or "wrong" way to do corporate worship. What we learn from the Psalms about this topic is wide-ranging in its application yet imprecise in terms of styles of corporate worship.

Here are a few clues about worship by believers in God a few thousand years ago.

• "Come, let us bow down in worship" (Psalm 95:6). They bowed down back then! It doesn't mean we have to, for this is not a principle. It is an inspired historical note, yet the important concept it teaches us is the reverence and awe we should have when we worship our holy God. Truly, that means different things to different worship groups, but the key is that we stand (or bow) in awe of a God who deserves our utmost worship.

• "Come, let us sing for joy to the LORD; let us shout aloud to the Rock of our salvation" (v. 1). They sang worship songs, just as we do! When you sing for joy and shout aloud, you know a couple of things. You're not in 1965 anymore, and you're probably not in a Baptist church. (I'm kidding. I'm a Baptist, and yes, we do sing for joy!) The point here is that worship of our amazing and incomprehensibly almighty God comes from a heart full of wonder and admiration! We worship not for how it makes us feel but for how it reflects God's greatness.

• "Let us go to his dwelling place, let us worship at his footstool" (Psalm 132:7). Here is what that footstool reference is all about: God is seated on His throne in heaven, and in a metaphorical sense His feet are resting on a footstool called earth. That allows us to picture that we are worshiping at God's feet. It might even remind us of the Mary-Martha-Jesus incident in the New Testament, when Martha was so busy serving her guests that she forgot to worship the Lord, who was in the house. Like Mary, we worship when we enjoy Jesus's presence and allow Him to teach us through His Word.

• "Worship the LORD in the splendor of his holiness" (Psalm 96:9). Our worship is not about us, not about our preferences, not even about our style. It is about our heavenly Father. To worship Him in the splendor of His holiness is to see Him with an awe that we reserve for nothing else. It is to see Him in His majestic and inspiring glory. And it is to recognize His perfect holiness.

As that concept of God comes into view through our worship, we begin to relax about life's troubles, and we begin to recognize that God stands for what is right and true. We grow to understand that His decisions about our lives are always right and based on His holiness. In that reality, which we learn about in God's sanctuary, God will always do what is right and true in regard to us and others.

We peek back to Psalm 1, and we see how life will all play out eventually: "The LORD watches over the way of the righteous, but the way of the wicked leads to destruction" (v. 6). That truth is discovered in the sanctuary of delighting in the law of the Lord (see v. 2), a worship practice of the blessed person.

Climbing Songs

Sometimes when soldiers are marching along—burdened down with their weapons and their backpacks—they sing. Perhaps they sing a well-known song, or maybe they chant an old march that has historical significance for their branch of the military. *The Daily Telegraph* newspaper once reported online that segments of the Russian army sang the theme to the cartoon show *SpongeBob SquarePants* as they trudged along.

That image may take a couple moments to sink in, but in an odd way, it does verify my point.

Traveling a long road with others, it appears, can be made more tolerable with singing.

In Old Testament days, one of the key marches undertaken by the Jewish people was the trek to Jerusalem for worship. There were three primary events that drew the Hebrews to the Holy City: Passover, Pentecost, and the Feast of Tabernacles. As the pilgrims made the journey to the City of David, some had to travel for three or four days. But no matter where they came from, they all had to go up—up to the hill on which Jerusalem is located.

And as the people made their way along the roads to Jerusalem, they sang a number of different songs, all with infinitely more value and power than a cartoon theme song.

These climbing songs are called the Songs of Ascent, and they are found in Psalm 120 through Psalm 134. Each has a different theme and different content, and we can learn something about the worshiping life by examining these ancient songs.

Today we don't worship as the Hebrews in Old Testament times did, nor do we generally travel in groups to church. But as we examine these snapshots of worship preparation from a different era, we can be challenged anew to find deep and lasting value in the many aspects of giving our praise and worship to God. These songs can spur us on to a better understanding of what the worshiping life can mean to our relationship with God.

Psalm 120. We worship a God who hears us and answers us when we are in distress. In this case, the pilgrims are praying about the problem of being falsely accused. We don't worship an impersonal God; we worship One who reacts individually to our specific needs. *How else can we respond but to bow down?*

Psalm 121. The pilgrims look up at the hills of Jerusalem with anticipation, and they are reminded of the source of their help: "the LORD, the Maker of heaven and earth" (v. 2). How can we resist worshiping One who can fling the universe into existence with His voice yet still cares enough that He watches over us? "The LORD watches over you. . . . The LORD will watch over your coming and going both now and forevermore" (vv. 5, 8). *What else can we do but respond in awe?*

Psalm 122. Excitedly, the Hebrew pilgrims enter the city and then the temple with anticipation, rejoicing (v. 1). They respect what the city of Jerusalem stands for, and they desire its safety. They embrace the experience of having a place to worship, of having a legacy of God's care, and of having the responsibility of praying for its peace. How closely does that resemble our anticipation as we visit our house of worship? *Can their excitement and their challenge spur us to holy anticipation of our worship times?*

Psalm 123. The pilgrims look past the City of David, and they lift up their eyes toward heaven. They remind us to elevate our thinking above the mundane and contemplate the divine. It is in peering with our mind's eye into the realm of our God that we remember His mercy and His help when those around us seek to bring us trouble. A heavenly view protects us from succumbing to the problems that surround us. *Don't the glories of heaven outshine the difficulties of earth?*

Psalm 124. Every people group has stories, but the stories of the Hebrews are unlike any other. As they march toward worship, looking toward Jerusalem, they also look back—figuratively. They look back to the remembrances of a people rescued and preserved by God's hand. They sing then as we do now, "Our help is in the name of the LORD" (v. 8). *Can we perceive that no matter which way we look, we can see God's provision, which brings us to an attitude of worship?*

Psalm 125. The mountains come back into view, this time as a metaphor for the endurance of God's people and the encompassing protection of God. The image is as old as the hills, but the application to us is as modern as today. God's love and care for His people never changes, and as Psalm 73 reminds us, those who don't follow God will not prevail. *Doesn't the protection of our Father and the permanence of our faith make us want to sing God's praises?*

Psalm 126. Perhaps we cannot understand the emotions being expressed here as the people recall a time of exile and return, but we can imagine their joy. This psalm again demonstrates God's practical help, to which the people respond with songs of joy (v. 5). *Can we stop and praise God for His tender care to the returning exiles then, and pray for all those in our world who are being exiled from their homes because of political strife?*

Psalm 127. Celebrate the family! Even as the people march toward the temple, they praise God for his plan of putting them in family units. Ideas such as hard work and God's love and the heritage of children are all considered in this family edition of the Songs of Ascent. *Do we petition heaven often enough on behalf of our families?*

Psalm 128. "Family Edition: The Sequel." Valuable lessons for the family is the theme of this song: fear of God, walking in God's ways, labor and prosperity, well-being of family members. Again the family is lifted up and promises are made. Hebrew families then and Christian families today worship God by living His way. *As we worship, should we praise God for both family and His clear directions for family life?*

Psalm 129. Darkness descends. Perhaps this song is sung in a minor key as it depicts oppression and hate that was hurled at Zion, this beloved city. It is a contemplation of darker times when the enemies of the Hebrews brought trouble. *Aren't there times when our prayers are deeply serious petitions about troubling, worrisome times? That's worship too.*

Psalm 130. Starting in the depths but rising to the heights of God's forgiveness and promise of hope, this song surely brings encouragement to the people. The singers speak of a need for mercy, for the dissolution of sin's penalty, and they receive just what they need! *Isn't it true that worship is not always joyful exuberance; sometimes it is an expression from a troubled heart, but then we find the joy of hope in God!*

Psalm 131. How important for a group of people or for individuals to recognize that this life and its answers are not about us. We cannot understand life without God's knowledge and help. He is our hope. *In our worship, even if we don't go to our knees physically, we should bow with our hearts before God and realize that He is our only hope.*

Psalm 132. If only they had video! Imagine the scene as the people gather to dedicate the temple or to see a new king crowned!

With no video, this musical recollection will have to do. David is the human center of this song, for it relates to him, but the true central character in this remembrance of a highlight in Jerusalem's history is "the Mighty One of Jacob" (v. 2). *How can our stories of God's work lead us to send Him praise and worship?*

Psalm 133. Thank you, David. We need this reminder. You valued the unity of your people, and you remind us of something vital: we must have brothers and sisters in Christ who are willing to use Jesus-like humility and set aside personal agendas so our churches can worship and serve as one body. *Indeed, do we know how good and pleasant it is when brothers and sisters live together in unity?*

Psalm 134. It's getting rather specific here: thanks for all the people who work in the temple. For the Hebrews, worship depends on the cooperation of a number of people from various tribes working together to allow the temple to run properly. It's not hard to make the connection to our churches today. *How often do we pray for and thank God for and ask for assistance for all the people in our churches "who minister . . . in the house of the LORD" (v. 1)?*

Psalm 135. Cue the praise team! This song would fit right in today. It is a praise song. It proclaims glory to God for His goodness, for His greatness, for His sovereignty, for His creativity, and for His many deeds on behalf of the Hebrews. We would have to tack a lot of praise songs together to match Psalm 135. *Isn't it good to sing praises to our God in worship?*

It's been perhaps three thousand years since the psalms that speak of worship were written. It's pretty amazing, isn't it, that what they praised and worshiped God for can fit into categories that closely match what we praise and worship Him for!

Methods have changed. Today we would take a bus to the temple (or our own car, if there was parking near the Temple Mount).

We would play different instruments than they used (imagine a Fender Stratocaster in the temple!). Their circumstances were far different from ours.

Yet when we go into the sanctuary of God (see chap. 9), don't we do so with exactly the same purposes the Hebrews had? We take along our problems so we can learn to look at them in a new, more God-centered way. We look at our past and praise God for His direction. We look ahead and ask God for His guidance. We look around at our families and praise God for them.

We worship. It's what the Hebrews did long ago in the days when the psalms were written, and we desire today to enjoy the worshiping life as another component of living the Psalms life.

F i v e

The Bible-Based Life

When was the last time a book took you by storm, over-whelming you with its insights or drama or information? When has a book left you breathless with its soaring prose or its I-can't-put-it-down suspense?

I recently read a book that drew me in and pulled me along because it had, waiting somewhere inside, a personal connection to our family. I eagerly read page after page to find that part of the tome with a link to my father, a member of the Greatest Generation.

The title of the work is *An Army at Dawn* by Rick Atkinson. In his well-researched book, Atkinson tells the long and complicated story of American fighting forces in North Africa during World War II. It is a compelling record of successes and failures for the soldiers and their leaders, but that alone was not what hooked me.

Toward the end of this historical account, as Atkinson writes in riveting detail about the American soldiers moving through the campaign against the Germans in Tunisia, my excitement grew. It was not because I enjoyed reading about the mess that is war but because I knew the armies were moving toward a specific location that has a unique place in our family's story. Excitedly, I finally arrived, along with the narrative, at a dusty outcropping in the deserts of Tunisia. It was at that point in the book that I read with fascination, horror, and a heart swelling with pride the story that my dad could never bear to tell—the story of the Battle of Hill 609. Reading those pages, I began to understand for the first time in my life what my dad, Second Lieutenant John C. Branon, went through to help protect our country.

With tears in my eyes, I caught a glimpse of the danger, fear, and chaos my dad faced as he led his men on that hill. I half expected Atkinson to mention 2nd Lt. Branon as one of the brave Americans who was shot and seriously wounded during that noisy, bloody battle. Yes, as I read those pages, I was immersed in the fateful and unforgettable day when my dad won his Purple Heart and nearly died on Hill 609.

A book brought to life for me in a way I could never experience any other way the heroic efforts of my father!

Books can do that. They can open our hearts and encourage our spirits in uncountable ways. But generally speaking, we all have different preferences and find different outcomes as we select the books that appeal individually to us.

However, there is a singularly important book that can touch the heart of each of us in the deepest and most profound way because it has a direct connection to all of us. This book has both a universal appeal and a universal application. It does not matter what your background might be, what your interests are, or what your heritage is. This book has answers for people of all ethnic groups, all social strata, and all political or religious preferences.

Of course, the book I have in mind is the Bible. In the section of it that we are contemplating here—the Psalms—we find continual reminders that the life lived according to what we read in this remarkable book is better than any other life a person might attempt to cobble together. It shows and tells us that the Psalms life presents the opportunity to enjoy a Bible-based life—a life informed by, guided by, and solidified by the teachings and the doctrines and the principles of this Book of books.

We must, of course, realize that when Psalm 119 was written, the words it references—God's words—did not include the entire canon of Scripture as we know it. However, we do know that when later books were added to the canon, they came to be included in all references to God's words. For instance, 2 Timothy 3:16 includes both the books of the New Testament and the books of the Old Testament as inspired writings that are valuable for our teaching.

I may find *An Army at Dawn* to be special because my dad's life-changing story is found in its pages, but that historical masterpiece (it won a Pulitzer Prize) cannot begin to have the all-encompassing, eternal importance of God's Book. In the pages of the Bible, we find timeless and essential truth for all people. Inspired by the God who designed and created both our world and us as its inhabitants, the Bible explains what God expects of us and how we can best interact with Him as our God and with each other as cotravelers in this life.

In a sense, we can find in one particular, amazing section of the Psalms our ultimate guide to the vitality of God's Word in our lives, for it spells out in a multitude of ways what the Bible does for us and how we are to respond to it. It shouldn't surprise us that it takes the longest chapter in the Bible—Psalm 119— to detail for us these helpful interactions. This fact by itself helps us to appreciate how much God values our understanding of His teachings, and it should challenge us to dig deeply into His Book. If we want to live as the Psalms tell us to live, we must, as the psalmist says in 119:15, "meditate on [God's] precepts and consider [His] ways."

There is something thrilling to discover in the pages of Psalm 119 as you work your way through it in an effort to mine its truth. You'll be excited to learn that nearly every one of its verses mentions God's Word in one way or another. By my rather amateurish count, I found this to be true in 170 of the 176 verses! If you need proof that God wants us to value the truths of His inspired standards in the Bible, this chapter certainly provides it.

Those 170 or so verses use a variety of terms to represent God's truth: *laws, statutes, decrees, word, commands,* and *precepts* are the most prevalent. So as you begin to explore this chapter, you will find a nearly endless array of truths or challenges or instructions regarding how the words of God's Book are meant to inform our lives.

One suggestion I would make as we begin to unfold how to live by Psalm 119 is to grab a notebook and a pen and your Bible. Make three columns on your paper. Write "Verse" above one column, "Synonym for God's Word" above the middle column, and "Command, Request, or Teaching" above the third column. As you have time, start filling in the blanks, beginning with verse 1. Word of caution: it might take several sheets of paper and more than a little time to work your way through this exciting task.

As you begin, your columns may look like something like this.

Verse	Synonym for God's Word	Command, Request, or Teaching
1	"law of the LORD"	walk according to . . . leads to blessedness
2	"statutes"	keep them and seek God . . . leads to blessedness

You will be in awe of what God's Word teaches as you continue the study.

Whether or not you carry through with that project, the important thing to understand is what this vital chapter can reveal to us about how to live. In a way, it's an instruction manual for what to do with the mighty book of Scriptures you have in your hand. Finding a key to understanding the Bible is hard for many Christians to do. We may listen to great teaching, we may read from a devotional book, or we may listen to good Christian music based on biblical truths, but we may not know what the Bible is really telling us until we dig in and discover for ourselves its valuable principles and then attempt to live by them.

Psalm 119 can help us with that.

To begin thinking about the value of living the Bible-based life, let's look at one of the words you will find if you do the dissection of the chapter as mentioned previously. In fact, it's the term used in verse 1: *law*. This word is used in as many as forty of the verses of Psalm 119. We begin with this word because of its importance both in a Bible-based life and in all of life. It is a word that speaks to us of authority.

Stop and think a moment about the number of laws that are on the books in the United States—just the federal laws that have been passed in the nation's long history. One source I read suggested that there are more than twenty thousand laws *just about guns*. Twenty thousand laws telling the citizens of the USA how to buy, sell, own, use, and discard guns! In all, according to another source, there may be upwards of three hundred thousand laws on record in the United States' federal code. As one person put it, you are probably breaking a law right now and don't even know it. (I promise not to turn you in if you don't snitch on me.)

While the United States' legislature has the authority to make laws—and it seems there is no end to that process—only God has the authority to make the laws we really need regardless of where we live. God is the ultimate lawgiver, and that means He expects us to strive toward an understanding of His laws and our responsibility to them.

The term *law* as used in Psalm 119 has a dual meaning. First, it reflects the commands given in Scripture, whether individual directives or entire groupings such as the Ten Commandments. And second, the term can refer to the entire canon of what we call the Bible. Bible scholar Derek Kidner says *law* "can be used of a single command . . . or again of Scripture as a whole."[1] Another way to think about the application of the term *law* might be to think of it as God's will: what is it God wants us to do?

As we look at how God's Word is reflected in the word *law* in Psalm 119, we can categorize into three sections what we are being taught.

- Obeying God's laws
- The positive aspects of those laws
- How the wicked respond to God's laws

Let's look at these ideas one at a time.

1. Obeying God's Laws

I have noticed a growing tendency, in many Christian circles today, to deemphasize the need to obey God's laws. Some people contend that believers should not teach that the Christian life is a list of rules to be followed. This is a natural response to the legalism that marked so much of American Christianity in an earlier generation. Christians made up a bunch of rules to determine a person's spirituality. If you followed those manmade rules, you were somehow more spiritual than those who didn't.

I've tried unsuccessfully to explain one such extrabiblical standard to my students at the Christian university where I have been
an adjunct professor for many years. To illustrate the importance
of writing about things that are timely and relevant, I tell them of
an antiquated "no beards" rule. This was a part of the rulebook
of many Christian colleges during the 1960s and 1970s, the era
of Vietnam, nascent rock music, and social unrest. When I try
to explain to my students that beards meant rebellion against the
government or authority or parents, they look at me as if I were
telling them that the earth is flat.

As an overreaction to the sometimes ridiculous rules the church
used to saddle its members with in that generation, the current
paradigm is to suggest that it's good to have no rules. But that
approach contradicts the clear teaching of God's Word just as
much as making too much of manmade rules contradicts God's
grace and love. The things that God has told us to avoid, or the
guidelines He has given us for doing His work on earth, are flawless, beneficial, and worthy of our attention.

It is to our advantage, as followers of the King, to seek out God's
standards and use them as our guide through life.

Let's examine a sampling of verses that encourage us to do just
that. We will look at three verses to provide an overview of reasons
why we seek to obey the standards presented in the Bible. Clearly,
the Bible is so much more than a book of guidelines and rules, but
these are a part of its overall thrust, and we should take its principles seriously.

• Psalm 119:1: "Blessed are those whose ways are blameless, who
walk according to the law of the LORD."

Living blamelessly. It's easy to say that being blameless in life
is its own reward, and that would be true. But it also has other

benefits that go beyond just feeling good about yourself. In Genesis 6:9 we read, "This is the account of Noah and his family. Noah was a righteous man, blameless among the people of his time, and he walked faithfully with God." In an age marked by lawlessness, ungodliness, and enough debauchery to cause God to send a deadly deluge, Noah stood out! He was described in this verse with a word that is translated in other places in the Bible as "upright," "perfect," "whole," and "without blemish."

For his adherence to righteousness, Noah was singled out and saved from the coming destruction of the rest of mankind! Because he was blameless, he got to be the patriarch of the new generations of humanity that would follow the big flood.

Noah wasn't alone. Abraham was told to be blameless (Genesis 17:1). Job was found to be blameless (Job 1:1). New Testament church leaders were instructed to be blameless (Titus 1:7). It's a mighty good thing to be found innocent of charges when it comes to the laws of God. In fact, Psalm 119:1 says it makes a person blessed.

But let's move things up a few thousand years and think of what it means to be blameless today. What does life look like for us if we want to emulate biblical characters who were labeled blameless?

To begin with, we are not talking about some kind of legalistic approach in which we set ourselves up as better than others. I have seen that backfire horribly in people who seemed to be a one-person Christian police force, only to get tripped up embarrassingly by their own sins. Blamelessness instead has a look of humility and confession, marked by the realization that we are all vulnerable to sin and must be willing and eager to acknowledge our wrongdoing.

A blameless believer takes care of the two-by-four in his own eye before pointing out the speck of sawdust in his neighbor's. A blameless Christian doesn't look for loopholes in God's clear standards in order to flaunt his own indiscretions. A blameless follower of Jesus delights in the purity of obedience, the freedom of godliness, and the joy of regret-free living. A blameless believer understands that he is not sinless nor perfect; he is eager to allow God's forgiveness to wash away sins and help him maintain a strong relationship with God.

• Psalm 119:34: "Give me understanding, so that I may keep your law."

Obeying with understanding. Sometimes we don't want to do something because we don't really understand why we should do it. I think that might have been a big part of my problem with math in high school. I was okay when we were doing stuff that I knew I would use later. Knowing how to multiply numbers together and get a product or divide them to get a dividend seemed to make great sense. I knew I would have to do that kind of thing to balance a checkbook or to figure out my batting average once I became shortstop for the Cincinnati Reds.

But then I moved along in math and ran into problems that had both numbers and letters in them. We started talking about theorems and postulates and other things that sounded like they belonged in a monastery or something. I apologize right now to my brother-in-law and daughter, who both taught math and even understood calculus, but these new kinds of math problems and situations did not seem to be anything I could ever use. I had no understanding of why we were attempting to solve for x, so I had no desire to follow those math rules.

I think there are many people who look at God's laws and feel the same way. They don't understand the positive aspects of God's standards, so they don't bother. They don't feel compelled to have a life set apart by godliness. With no understanding of why, they find it easy to live by their own standards of self-interest.

To get a glimpse at why obeying God's guidelines is so important, let's sneak over to the New Testament and look at the two top commandments Jesus told us to obey. First, He said we are to love God with all of our heart, soul, and mind. And second, He said we should love our neighbors as much as we love ourselves. (See Matthew 22:34–40.)

Imagine for a moment that you were someone who has not been touched by the reality of God's love, or that you've never even come to terms with the truth that God has created this world (see Romans 1:20). Let's say you've been raised with a God-free view of life and He has no role in your thinking.

If you were that person, you would have no reason to "keep," or obey, Jesus's teaching to love God with all of your being. "Why?" you would ask. "What has He ever done for me? I'm getting along just fine without Him. I have no feelings either way about God, so I'm not going to love Him."

Like me in trigonometry class, you have no why. You don't know of a good reason to follow Jesus's teaching.

But I'll assume that if you have gotten this far in this book, you are not that person. Instead you have been touched by the Holy Spirit, who convicted you of the sin in your life that alienated you from God. You realized by the Spirit's leading that you need a Savior, so you turned to Jesus in faith. You were redeemed.

This reality alone should leave you breathlessly in love with God! You know what Jesus has done for you and how much He loves you. It is easy for you, then, to have the understanding that Psalm 119:34 speaks of, making it easy to love God with all your heart. Also, once we understand God's grace and forgiveness to us, we should have nothing but pure and selfless love toward our neighbors—people God loves and wants to redeem as well.

It is our understanding of God's greatness, His gift of salvation, and His boundless love for us that compel us to "keep [God's] law and obey it with all [our] heart."

• Psalm 119:43: "I have put my hope in your laws."

Providing hope. Increasingly, we see what havoc is wreaked on our world by lawlessness. When a group of people decide that they have no reason to live by the standards society has set forth, hope disappears. We know that even man's laws, when they are just and when they are obeyed, allow people to live in hope.

Notice how many times the psalmist places hope in God's laws: "I have put my hope in your word" (vv. 74, 81, 114, 147).

When around us we see hopelessness and society on the edge of chaos, we can stand on the solid ground of God's laws. His standards give us hope that there is a reasonable, rational way to live. There is a stability to life that can come only as we live the way our Creator has asked us to live.

A few verses later in Psalm 119, we see a succession of ideas stemming from the idea of hope, and they remind us again of how hope and God's laws are intertwined. The psalmist says this: "Remember your word to your servant, for you have given me hope. My comfort in my suffering is this: Your promise preserves my life. The arrogant mock me unmercifully, but I do not turn from your law" (vv. 49–51).

Again we stand amazed at the teaching of this chapter.

Notice the sequence in this passage. In verse 49, God's servant finds hope in God's word. (This concept is repeated in verse 74, which says, "May those who fear you rejoice when they see me, for I have put my hope in your word." Even today we sense the excitement of a group of Christians who see another believer staking his or her hope on the teachings of Scripture. That is surely a celebratory moment now as it was then.)

We move to verse 50, which adds to the joy of hope found in God's word by reminding us of the comfort of God's promises.

Reality strikes in verse 51 as we see how those who have not been touched by God's miraculous and stupendous love respond to the working of God in a person's heart. They mock relentlessly the one rejoicing in hope and promise (how sad it is that the unredeemed seek purpose in mockery instead of in God), yet our human hero in this passage refuses to be swayed: "but I do not turn from your law."

Is this not a "Wow!" moment for us in this culture?

We need not fear those who as yet have not turned to Jesus, no matter what they say. We have hope, comfort, and the stability of the law to point us back to our faith and our dependence on God. Isn't that, in itself, another great reason to live the Bible-based life?

2. Positive Aspects of God's Laws

Think for a moment about how much you appreciate laws.

Isn't it fantastic that grocery stores must obey the rules enforced by the Department of Agriculture? Nobody wants to buy a gallon of milk at the store with the worry that that the milk might be older than your cat.

Isn't it great that some guy who left school after the eighth grade and can't even spell *duodenum* can't hang out a shingle and call himself a doctor?

Doesn't it make you feel good that somebody can't build a deck on the second floor of your house with balsa wood and airplane glue?

Laws are good! They keep a society from harm and danger,

and they keep good citizens from being swindled by not-so-good citizens.

Let's look at how Psalm 119 reveals the positive aspects of God's laws.

• Psalm 119:18: "Open my eyes that I may see wonderful things in your law."

Wonderful things. Did you ever stop to think how wonderful it is to live in a nation ruled by laws?

For instance, what a joy it is to drive across the United States and know that every time you come to a red traffic light, everyone knows that the law says stop. Have you ever driven in a country where obeying traffic lights is not even considered an option? They are ignored like a bad suggestion as drivers fly through intersections without the least bit of concern for what color the light is.

Isn't it nice to know that among the wonderful things the laws of an organized, well-run country provide are doctors who have medical degrees, guidelines for how food is to be prepared in restaurants, and standards for how your house should be built?

If we take a welcoming approach to the guidelines and laws God has given us in the Bible, life just simply goes better. As Psalm 119:39 says, "Take away the disgrace I dread, for your laws are good." And in Psalm 119:62, the writer says, "At midnight I rise to give you thanks for your righteous laws."

The righteous and good laws that God has placed throughout Scripture serve as guardrails to keep us on track both spiritually and with our fellow humans.

Remember those days in school—normally the first day of school each year—when the teacher spelled out for you and your friends the always popular classroom rules? Wasn't that fun? Didn't all of you sit with eager anticipation as some adult you hardly knew laid down the law for the next 180 school days?

- Don't chew gum. "Yes! I love that rule."
- All homework must be in on time. "All right! That is my kind of standard!"
- If you come to class without your textbook, you will be sent to the office. "All right! I *love* going to the office!"

Am I right about those reactions?

Of course not! Nobody wants to sit through a lecture about a bunch of rules, and nobody is going to cheer when a rule is announced. Instead we start looking for loopholes in the rules as fast as they escape our teacher's lips.

That's because we don't look at school rules or driving rules or employment rules with the same excitement we should have as we look at God's rules.

How else can we interpret the following verses but to call God's laws beautiful, righteous, and good? "The law of the LORD is perfect, refreshing the soul. The statutes of the LORD are trustworthy, making wise the simple. The precepts of the LORD are right, giving joy to the heart. The commands of the LORD are radiant, giving light to the eyes" (Psalm 19:7–8).

We don't love and obey God's laws so we can mark off some checklist of legalistic activity. Instead we love God in the way we serve and respect our spouse—as a show of selfless and other-directed love. To love God's law is to tell God that we trust His Word, that we have no other agenda but to serve Him, and that we recognize His greatness, majesty, and splendor. When we do, we show that we appreciate the positive aspects of His laws, which lead us to seek them out and obey them.

3. How the Wicked Respond to God's Laws

Sometimes it helps us to see the converse of something so we can understand its significance.

Think about your job, for instance. Let's assume all the normal situations are true for your job—you are planning to keep the job, you are making a decent salary, and you basically enjoy what you do.

What would happen if you were to report to work the next day and do the following: You sit at your desk all day and look at Facebook. You miss an important meeting because you don't want to bother. Your boss stops by to say hello, and you tell her you can't stand her voice and ask her to just go away.

Of course, you would be called in to a little get-together with some significant people, and you might even find yourself being ushered out of the building with all of your personal items in a box tucked under your arm.

All of the activities mentioned on our "get me fired" day are the opposite of what you know is right and proper to do at your job. Somehow you know this, and you act accordingly. So on a normal day, you obey protocol, work hard, and ask your boss how her weekend went. And you live to pick up another paycheck.

Now let's look at life as we know it.

Many people meet God's laws with the same disdain our hypothetical scenario showed regarding workplace rules.

In Psalm 119, the psalmist realizes this and lets us in on how those who do not respect God's laws act. While we have just seen the hope and help we can enjoy through living God's way, life takes on a far different reality for those who adamantly reject the Creator's standards. Let's look at a few of the verses that point this out.

• Psalm 119:53: "Indignation grips me because of the wicked, who have forsaken your law."

Forsaking them. Have you ever heard the term "God-forsaken"? This seems to best describe those who turn their backs on God's standards. When we see lives being destroyed by ungodliness, this verse suggests, we can rightly be indignant. In fact, the King James Version translates the first part of this verse to say, "Horror hath taken hold upon me" as a result of what the ungodly do. It is not only the actions that appall us but also the *destiny* of the unsaved. We sorrow because we know that living the converse of the reality of salvation will lead to such a horrible eternal conclusion.

The truth of this verse is a reminder that we do not respond in horror at the actions of the unredeemed so we can cast aspersions at them and look down on them. The fact that they disobey God's standards and cause themselves undue difficulty should make us concerned about their spiritual well-being. The contrast between a life of forsaking God's standards and a life of obeying the Lord should motivate us to pray for and show loving concern for all who have forsaken God's law.

• Psalm 119:85: "The arrogant dig pits to trap me, contrary to your law."

Pitfalls ahead. Those who consciously live outside of God's standards may attempt to sway us to their way of thinking. They may seek to have us fall into their pits of despair.

We can think of several Bible stories that bear this out.

- Satan in the wilderness, trying to trick Jesus into sinning
- Potiphar's wife trying to lure Joseph into her bedroom
- Babylonian officials trying to influence Daniel to pray to the king

Those who work in opposition to the laws of God may try to

trick us into disobeying His guidelines, but if we keep in mind that God is always true, is always right, and never resorts to any kind of deception, we can more easily avoid those traps.

• Psalm 119:150: "Those who devise wicked schemes are near, but they are far from your law."

Schemes unlimited. As much as I love Jamaica, I realize that there is a problem in paradise. Crime in this country has everyone worried. Murders continue to climb, and incivility threatens to disrupt the lives of the millions of good people who live there.

One of the most troublesome problems this country faces stems from a greedy and wicked scheme that has influenced many to live a life dependent on crime. It is the lottery scam, in which people from this land call vulnerable people in another country and use false pretenses to trick them into sending money to them.

It is one of the most devious and evil nonviolent crimes in society, for it preys on those who are elderly and most vulnerable.

That is just one small example of what happens when people do not operate under God's standards but instead devise wicked schemes of one kind or another. No matter where they live and no matter what the sinful action, when someone finds a way to disobey God's laws—by coveting or lying or cheating or disrespecting God or stealing or hating others—that scheme draws the person farther and farther from God.

But let's not look disapprovingly at others. Let's move to the next verse instead and camp there: "Yet you are near, Lord, and all your commands are true" (v. 151). That is our sincere and redeeming hope when we see the evil that wicked schemes can bring on our fellow humans.

We cannot, in this short chapter, exhaust the teachings of Psalm 119 about God's Word and its value to us. It might take a lifetime to mine all the nuggets of truth from this long and exciting book. May this chapter be just the beginning of a great adventure of renewing a call to live the Bible-based life.

S i x

The Secure Life

Security is a major issue today, both on a personal level and on a governmental level. In 2017, the United States launched an aircraft carrier that cost thirteen billion dollars. How much money is that? Well, if you had started counting by ones in AD 782 and continued without stopping, you would have reached thirteen billion in 2017, about the time the USS *Gerald R. Ford* aircraft carrier was christened. That's a rather large expense to help secure the United States from outside forces, but we all know how valuable national security happens to be.

On a more personal level, to be secure in today's world, we do a lot of unusual things. We take off our shoes and belts in the airport. We put cameras inside our own houses. We set aside some of our hard-earned money every two weeks and put it in a savings account we may or may not use decades later. We have more passwords for our online activity than we can keep track of. And we may even take lessons on how to use a gun.

Certainly, there are a variety of things we can do as we seek to live securely in an often insecure world. But if we want to narrow down our choices from the multitude of things that *might* bring us security to the one thing that is *guaranteed* to make us truly secure, we will turn to Psalm 46. In this short passage, written by "the Sons of Korah," we will discover the most dependable source of help available in the face of the crises that interrupt our lives, affect our family's well-being, and cause us to lose sleep.

Before we take a deeper look into Psalm 46 to see how we can find security, let's examine some of the major problems that can lead to insecurity in our world.

Perhaps this listing doesn't pinpoint your main concern as you seek security, but one can surmise that all of us who claim to be followers of Jesus Christ encounter some of these issues to one degree or another.

Questions about faith itself. How can this not be a major concern as we notice what seems to be an effort to destroy the confidence we have in the gospel story and all that goes with it? Some seem to be looking for ways to discount the importance of the Bible, downplay the role of the Christian church, and devalue God's role in our world. This leads to a growing problem of Christians being marginalized, sometimes even persecuted for their beliefs. I witnessed an example of this soon after the death of Billy Graham in 2018. Before the great evangelist could even be buried, I saw numerous headlines of articles that appeared to be trying to destroy the reputation of one of the most admired men in America.

The more this happens to Christians who do not grasp the importance of the security offered by passages like Psalm 46, the more likely it is that those believers will drift off into a life stripped of its spiritual strength. If our belief is questioned enough, we may begin to shrink back from faithfulness and live in a way that is no different from the lives of those who don't claim to know Jesus Christ.

Trouble with finances. The nagging irritation of financial difficulties, which tends to sap the energy of people who are struggling and pits family members against each other, is clearly a destroyer of security. No one feels secure when the mortgage is unpaid, when school loans strangle the budget, or when the resources to properly support the household can't be found. Christians sometimes feel an added weight of burden in financial crises because they know God has promised a fulfilling life, and that sometimes gets confused with financial security. There is not much in life that creates more insecurity in our day-to-day existence than having trouble with finances.

Interpersonal rifts. Think about one of those times in life when you've just had a seemingly unsolvable difference of opinion with your spouse or someone else you are close to, and then you have to go to work or some other formal function. It's hard to concentrate on anything other than the problem you left behind, isn't it? Enduring an interpersonal rift is a security robber of the first order.

Certainly, reality is harsh in all of these situations. Security is threatened when these crises—or others—dominate our lives. We long for anything that will give us hope that we can again dwell under an umbrella of protection, that we can wake up in the morning with a calm heart and a strong sense that today will be better. We pray for something to make us feel safe.

We don't know what situation led the writers of Psalm 46 to pen their song, and that might be to our benefit. Since the powerful words of this passage are not tied to a specific scenario, it might be easier for us to apply its teaching to any situation we face. Psalm 46 becomes a kind of one-passage-fits-all encouragement for any and all situations that sap our confidence and threaten our security.

So bring along your own insecurities—your own crises—and let's see how the words written for the director of music (see the psalm's introduction) can create for us a symphony of hope and safety that will lift our hearts and create a more stable reality for us.

Security Factor One: Security Comes through God's Dependability and His Word

Who doesn't love a place of refuge, a safe place to settle into where life's arrows cannot penetrate and where fear is swallowed up in security?

In 2016, a woman and her boyfriend were hiking in the snowy New Zealand wilderness when they lost track of trail markers that had been guiding them. As they struggled to return to civilization, the man fell to his death, leaving the woman to fend for herself in the middle of winter. She spent three fruitless days looking for a route back to safety. Then she discovered an abandoned cabin.

It became her refuge.

She survived in that cabin for a month before rescuers finally found her. That refuge was her only hope amid the cold, the wind, the snow, and the certain death she would have faced without it.

We too can get lost as we make our way through the world, making it necessary for us to seek a refuge. So we turn to Psalm 46:1, and there it is: "God is our refuge and strength, an ever-present help in trouble." Our refuge is the source of our security in crisis.

What makes God our refuge?

To begin with, he is singularly dependable as our safe place to run to when trouble strikes. It is to God, and God alone, we can turn with utter confidence no matter what the troubling circumstance might be. He is, as Martin Luther so fittingly wrote, "a mighty fortress" and a bulwark that never fails. In attempting to put into song the concepts of this, his favorite psalm, Luther—writing nearly five hundred years ago—captured the solution to the fears of our heart today when he wrote, "Our helper He amid the flood of mortal ills prevailing."

Only God—this mighty fortress, this strong tower of protection—can hide us in His mighty arms when we feel we are about to be overrun by today's "mortal ills." He can do that because He has provided us with a truth that will prevail over any and all of mankind's modern-day philosophies.

Notice, for instance, what Psalm 18:30 says. "As for God, his way is perfect: the LORD's word is flawless; he shields all who take refuge in him." There it is again: refuge. Except in this verse, we see an additional reality attached to it—a truth that can give us hope as we look around and realize that society seems to be very ill. Actions, words, and concepts that society once considered to be clearly beyond the barriers of morality are now presented as normal. The "mortal ills prevailing" that Luther wrote about grow more and more sickening.

Yet in the face of that—as we might feel insecure about our place in the world while we try to uphold strong biblical standards regarding how we live and interact—we have a dependable place of safety to make us secure. We have the word of the Lord, which is flawless and dependable as a guide for truth. In the Bible we have a shield—a refuge. Because we have the inspired Word of our God as our guide for faith and practice, and the internal guidance of the Holy Spirit to instruct us in what the Word says, we have security that as long as we live by its precepts, we are protected from the incorrect teachings of our society.

There is something else that is basic to this concept of God as our refuge—another concept pinpointed by Psalm 18. In verse 2, we read this: "The LORD is my rock, my fortress and my deliverer; my God is my rock, in whom I take refuge, my shield and the horn of my salvation, my stronghold."

The ultimate refuge we find in our heavenly Father is the combination of truth and realities that come to us from God's Word. Here is how Albert Barnes, the nineteenth-century American theologian, explained this truth: "The 'horn' is to animals the means of their defense. Their strength lies in the horn. Hence, the word is used here, as elsewhere, to represent that to which we owe our protection and defense in danger; and the idea here is, that God was to the psalmist what the horn is to animals, the means of his defense."[1]

As the provider of our salvation and the defender of those who are in the faith, God takes special care of us as we make our way through life. As His purchased ones through Jesus's death on the cross, we know that simply in belonging to Him, we are shielded by His mighty power and His love.

Let's talk about this in the most practical terms. Here are a couple of things God protects us from.

The dangers of temptation. Temptation surrounds us like a fog sometimes, tantalizing us with what seem to be inviting choices. This is not something that happens only to weak Christians. Temptation is common to man (see 1 Corinthians 10:13). It relentlessly pursues us all. It even tried to chase down the most uncommon man, Jesus.

Here's how the enticement works, according to James 1: we are dragged away and enticed. It's as if Satan gets us into his corner and offers us evil in a most inviting package. James says, "After desire has conceived, it gives birth to sin" (v. 15). Before it gets to that point, though, we need to recall that we have a refuge against that sin. "God is faithful," Paul reminds us, "he will not let you be tempted beyond what you can bear" (1 Corinthians 10:13). The enticement can be overcome with God's help because "he will also provide a way out so that you can endure it" (v. 13).

That's the power of a refuge. We may feel cornered by the Enemy's enticing offer, but he never has the power to make us sin. God is there to rescue us through the Holy Spirit, providing a safe passage away from the dangers of sinful behavior.

The terrors of abandonment. As a redeemed child of God, you are never alone. When you run into the refuge that God offers, you are not running into an empty building. The woman in New Zealand faced that frightening scenario, and she somehow survived. We have it even better. Our refuge is personal, and He stands with us in whatever trials we face.

Think for a moment about how alone Joshua must have felt as he took the reins of power from Moses when God's people reached the end of their epic desert crossing. A daunting task still lay ahead for the Israelites. They had to enter the promised land in the face of monumental dangers. Logistically and spiritually and militarily, Joshua faced a nearly impossible job.

That's why Deuteronomy 31:6 stands out as a beacon of hope, both for Joshua those thousands of years ago and for us today. He may have felt alone as he took over for the great leader Moses, but God assured him that he was not. The great Refuge was right beside him.

"Be strong and courageous," He told Joshua. "Do not be afraid or terrified because of [the enemy], for the LORD your God goes with you; he will never leave you nor forsake you" (Deuteronomy 31:6).

And before you assume that this was some Old Testament

teaching that was focused on Joshua alone, don't forget that the inspired New Testament writer reprised this amazing promise in Hebrews 13:5: "Never will I leave you; never will I forsake you." Then he added a little warmth to it by reminding us that we can confidently say, "The Lord is my helper; I will not be afraid" (v. 6).

Are you facing a task that has you overwhelmed? You are not alone.

Do you feel that others don't understand you? You are not alone.

Has grief made you feel like the world is now a foreign place? You are not alone.

But how accessible is this promised refuge?

He is an ever-present help.

This is good news, because in today's world, we want whatever we want or need to be delivered right now.

We may not yet have drones dropping off our online purchases five minutes after we order them, but we do have a got-to-have-it-now mentality. We can drive through and pick up our pizza. We can make airline reservations online and print off our boarding passes immediately. We can watch many of our favorite TV programs or movies on demand.

And we can get access to our eternal Father at a moment's notice.

Who can top the story found in Daniel 9 for immediate service? It almost takes your breath away to realize how quickly Daniel got a response to his request in that chapter.

As Daniel was praying to the Lord about the promised end of the Israelites' captivity, God gave him an immediate answer in the form of an angelic visitation. The angel Gabriel was dispatched from heaven when Daniel began talking, and before he could finish praying, the angel was in Daniel's presence.

That's the way it is with this promise.

God is an ever-present help in times of trouble. He may not

send a solution to our problem immediately, but the moment we cry out to Him, He always provides His comforting presence, His infallible truth, and His unchallenged promise of ultimate victory.

In 2017, Joni Eareckson Tada passed the fifty-year mark since she dove into shallow water as a teenager and came out a quadriplegic. She has been a remarkable example of someone who recognized God as an ever-present help in her trouble, even though God never healed her and allowed her to walk again. In an interview for *Christianity Today*, she said, "I'm amazed that the last 50 years feel like only 'a little while.' Maybe God does that when we finally do love Jesus more, when we finally do follow him more closely. Maybe he erases all the horror, all the despair, all the depression of the past when we learn how to trust God. He pushes into the background all the terrible times of anguish, and he brings forward the highlights—the moments of hope, peace, and growth. As I look back over 50 years, I just see God at work. That's pretty exciting."[2]

Whether our trouble lasts fifty years or just a little while, we have God's promise that He will be our ever-present help—our refuge—through it all.

Security Factor Two: Security Comes through the Comfort of God's Help

We had three of our grandchildren at our house overnight as their parents were on a weekend getaway. My wife, Sue, was at work that night, so I was on duty.

After the kids were in bed, I was in my office (probably watching the Detroit Tigers on TV) when a storm rumbled through our area. The rains and the thunder seemed just about to subside when suddenly a monstrously loud thunderclap exploded very near our house. This awakened the two girls, Eliana and Kaitlyn, but not

Logan, their brother. I first checked on Kaitlyn, who was two and a half, and I told her that it was just a loud boom and that it was over. I told her it was nothing to worry about. Eliana, ten, came rushing into the room in tears, telling me how scared she was because of the thunder.

To my surprise, little Kaitlyn piped up and said to her big sister, "It's okay, Eliana (yes, she could pronounce *Eliana* at age two), it was just a loud boom. It's nothing to worry about."

I couldn't believe it. This little punkin' was comforting her big sister with the exact words I had told her just a minute earlier. Eliana saw immediately that if her little sis was okay, she didn't have to worry so much either.

Comfort. It comes in all shapes and sizes, and we all need it. It is one of the most effective sources of security we know in life. No matter what our fear or how dangerous our situation, the discovery of comfort amid our insecurity warms our hearts and buoys us.

It's the understanding voice of a spouse who reminds us that no matter what our situation, "we're in this together, and we can overcome."

It's the wise parent who sits down with a teenager struggling at school and says, "You know, I've been through this too, and I'll do whatever it takes to help you make it."

It's the calming assurance from an employer who takes aside his overwhelmed employee and says, "I know how hard it is to learn this job, but together we're going to make this work."

It's the brilliant high school coach who puts his arm around the quarterback who just threw an interception and says, "You're my guy out there. I believe in you, and I know that next time you won't throw into double coverage."

And it is David, in Psalm 46, telling us, "There is a river whose streams make glad the city of God, the holy place where the Most High dwells. God is within her, she will not fall; God will help her at break of day" (vv. 4–5).

It's a comforting image, this river that makes glad the city of God. But back up one verse and see that as the writers describe trouble and trials, they paint a different watery scenario. There, where we are given a picture of disaster that we can handle fearlessly because of our great refuge, we see waters roaring and foaming.

Dangerous, raging seas give way to life-giving waters in God's presence.

What an inviting analogy the psalmists offer to remind us how much better is the secure life of the one trusting in God's comfort than the roiling, turbulent, angry oceans of those who depend on themselves and do not enjoy the refuge God offers.

Security Factor Three: Security Comes through Deliverance by God's Power

If you are a football fan, you know all about the remarkable record of the New England Patriots after Tom Brady took over as the team's quarterback. Between 2001 and 2017, this powerful team finished first in the AFC East in every year but one and won five Super Bowls. We could go on and on listing their remarkable accomplishments during Brady's career.

The point here is that if someone were to suggest that Tom Brady, who had a hard time breaking into the starting lineup as a college quarterback at the University of Michigan, wasn't all that good, all you would have to say is, "Look at his record."

End of argument.

That's a little like what the psalmists are saying about God in Psalm 46:8: "Come and see what the LORD has done." Just a little later in the Psalms, another writer says nearly the same thing:

"Come and see what God has done, his awesome deeds for mankind!" (Psalm 66:5).

Do you wonder if you can trust God—if you can depend on Him to be your deliverer in the midst of your trials and struggles?

Look at His record. While this passage zeroes in on the military victories God accomplished in Old Testament days, we have a larger sampling to choose from. Creator of the universe. Parter of the Red Sea. Raiser of the dead. Sustainer of all life. Things like that.

The mighty works of our powerful God remind us that He will always have the last word. Things will always turn out as He designed. Life is His creation, and He knows what the result will be, because He is sovereign over it.

He is the great deliverer, the provider of all that is good and right in this world. Whether He has to end wars peacefully or by His might (Psalm 46:9), it doesn't matter. He accomplishes what He needs to do.

Even today we see the works of the Lord manifested around the world.

• We see people who are steeped in the Muslim religion turn to Jesus Christ after having interactions that can only be explained as God-directed. With no contact with Christianity or even knowledge of it, they sense the importance of seeking out Jesus. A number of reputable books have documented these occurrences.

Here is an example of how this has happened, as told on the website *Lausanne World Pulse Archives*: "Dini . . . came to faith in Christ as a teenager in her native Indonesia. Feeling let down by family, friends and society and drifting into rebellion, Dini nonetheless yearned to know God and please him. On the night of Lailatur Qodar, when Muslims around the world make individualized prayers to Allah, Dini experienced a vision of Jesus Christ, who appeared before her and told her to follow him. Dini was hesitant. As a Muslim, she realized that following Christ would make her a Christian. But she overcame her fear and committed her life to Christ that same night. Peace filled her heart, even as persecution began."[3]

• We feel God's leading in our lives in direct ways. I recall this happening to my wife and me just after I graduated from college. I journeyed to the Philippines for six weeks on a basketball evangelism team. While in Manila, I visited a missionary kids' school, and as a freshly minted teacher, I was impressed. I sent a letter home to my wife, telling her that I felt God calling us to return to Faith Academy to teach. A couple of days later, I got a letter from her (written before she received mine), telling me that she felt God might be leading us to work at Faith. Boom! I already had a contract to teach that fall, so that gave us a year to plan our departure to Manila.

• We see how God raises up works for His glory. In 2017, our oldest daughter and her family (husband and daughter, age ten, and son, age seven) spent a little over a week in Guatemala at an organization started by one man, Carlos Vargas. He nearly died of an illness many years ago, but he felt that at that time God was going to allow him to live and start an important ministry. Today, Hope of Life has a huge campus in Guatemala where babies are rescued, downtrodden people are helped, and the gospel is presented. This is not a work one man could do alone; he could accomplish it only with God's direct help.

What has God done to provide for us, guide us, and deliver us?

Look at the record. It makes even Tom Brady's accomplishments look puny.

In the secure life, we have the confidence that our God—our deliverer God—has the power to do amazing things we can't even begin to fathom. What an encouragement that is! As we sit back and watch God work, we cannot help but marvel that He cares for us and even desires to have a relationship with us.

Security Factor Four: Security Comes through the Peace of God's Presence

Shhhh!

It's a quiet evening at home. Perhaps it's a cool summer night and the windows are open, letting in both the fresh air and the sound of crickets and other creatures of the night, serenading you with their steady song.

The TV is off, the computer is in sleep mode, and the cell phones have been silenced. You hold one of those old-fashioned contrivances—a book—in your hand, and you have a tall lemonade on the table next to you.

This is a good night. A quiet night. A relaxing night.

But one factor can make all the difference this evening.

If you are alone, there is a totally different atmosphere in the room. There is not the security, the completeness, or the pure satisfaction that could be enjoyed if you were to share it with a good friend or a close relative.

We are not made to be alone. And even an idyllic evening is better when shared with someone you love.

Psalm 16:11 says this: "You will fill me with joy in your presence." We truly complete the above picture when we mention that our Father is there with us.

In his book *Psalms*, Bible scholar Geoffrey W. Grogan writes of what might be called "the warm doctrine of God." He speaks of God's desire to be close to man even though He is majestic and all-powerful. And in the Psalms, man reciprocates that desire. Grogan suggests, "The great longing for God and his worship in psalms like 42, 43, 63, and 84 is really a longing for God himself."4 The writers of the psalms recognize how vital it is that we find our way into God's presence.

Listen to the following passage as it speaks of the amazing security we find in God. It evokes a feeling of protection and warmth that not even an inviting evening at home with our closest human companion can match: "I am always with you; you hold me by my right hand. You guide me with your counsel, and afterward you will take me into glory" (Psalm 73:23–24).

That is the security of being in God's presence.

The Real Life

It's about to get real.

The writers of the psalms that we sometimes call the Laments did not hold back. And I think we can identify.

In the train wreck that is the state of political discourse today, nobody seems able to show any restraint. Every offense, whether real or perceived, gets run out on the clothesline to flap in the breeze and distract the citizenry further and further from any hope of solutions.

It's a no-holds-barred arena where nobody seems to be happy with life as it is.

As modern as that concept seems, it is not too different from some of the entries we read in the book of Psalms. The writers of the portions of the Psalms that are called the Laments did not mince words as they poured out their hearts and expressed their viewpoints. The fact that those viewpoints seemed a little harsh when directed toward the one true and living God should not be lost on us. And the fact that these laments are part of the inspired

Word of God indicates that our heavenly Father wants us to read what we might today call "rants" written by several psalm writers.

As many as sixty-five psalms are considered laments—honest and bold expressions of discouragement and dismay that mix true angst over tough situations with a surprising intervention by the heavenly Father at the end. But in every case, we hear how one or more aspects of God's role in the writer's life is at first called into question.

The Lament Psalms could easily be called the Letters to the Editor. I'm not sure how many newspapers still print such letters anymore; our local newspaper does not because of a change in how the paper is structured these days. But in papers that do allow this kind of exchange between ordinary citizens and the people who read the news on newsprint, we get an idea about what is bothering folks.

One gentleman took issue with the road commission in his region because of what he felt were bad decisions about deer crossing signs. He wrote, "A lot of deer get hit by cars west of Crown Point on US 231. There are too many cars to have the deer crossing there. The deer crossing sign needs to be moved to a road with less traffic. —Tim"

Tim is lamenting the car-deer interactions, and although he might not quite grasp with logic and clarity the concept behind posting deer crossing signs, he has found a way to express his feelings.

Also, I like this letter to the editor from a woebegone but clever man named John about a recent article in his local newspaper: "Thank you very much for the helpful article about hoarding. I've put it with the others."

But mostly, letters to the editor are serious complaints people have about the condition of things in their city, state, or nation.

And similarly, the Laments are serious complaints about bad stuff happening to supposedly good people.

Let's listen in to hear what the writers are complaining about, and see if the answers they discover can help us find reason for contentment.

Laments generally fall into one of two categories: communal or personal. Sometimes the writer is representing a group of people and is voicing concerns they all have about an issue. At other times, the writer is expressing his own personal complaints. We will look at both kinds to get a better picture of how God wants us to keep it real and come to Him with what is truly on our heart.

Communal Lament 1: Psalm 12—Marginalized Faith

This psalm might make you wonder if some modern translator dropped this chapter into the Bible in, say, the first quarter of the twenty-first century, because its first few verses certainly don't sound like something written thousands of years ago. But it was penned by King David, who reigned in Israel in about 1000 BC.

So what he said, instead of being some anachronistic oddity that sounds too much like the twenty-first century to be an ancient Bible text, shows us this reality: people are the same today as they were back then.

Look at these words: "Help, LORD, for no one is faithful anymore; those who are loyal have vanished from the human race. Everyone lies to their neighbor; they flatter with their lips but harbor deception in their hearts" (vv. 1–2).

This makes me think of those Facebook postings that display some picture from the 1960s, perhaps a quaint photo of kids on a clearly unsafe playground or a family all sitting in the living room reading books, accompanied by a statement such as, "I'm glad I grew up when kids didn't stare at their cell phones all day." The implication is that there was a time in our social history not too long ago when everything was pretty close to idyllic, and woe is everyone who must endure living in this terrible new world we have created. It suggests that people were so different back in the day and that life then was all sunshine and popsicles.

In reality, people haven't changed, and the problems we see today are similar to the problems of the 1960s or even farther back, in the kingdom of Israel.

So the lament begins with a feeling that the people David had to deal with were ungodly, unfaithful, and full of lies.

Indeed, this is an uncomfortable situation for all of us who are trying to live godly lives, be faithful, and value truth. We can echo David's words today and bemoan the state of things. What we can't do is say that this day and age is worse than earlier ones, for as we have seen, this is a universal lament of believers down through the centuries. We are familiar with the New Testament Scriptures that tell us that all have sinned and there are really no righteous people in the world, reminding us of our need for God's amazing work of redemption and sanctification.

So, in this first part of the lament, we see the pattern of the Laments beginning to develop as David addresses God directly and as he spells out his complaint.

As is usually the case with a lament, David next petitions the Lord to do something about this situation. This makes sense to us, for we normally head this direction as well with our prayers of concern. How else can we respond to a wrong but to present God with our distress and then ask heaven for assistance?

David recognizes that it is up to God alone to redeem this situation—to stop those flattering lips of verse 2. It is God's role to silence those who, in mocking tones, say, "Who is lord over us?" (v. 4).

What happens next in this give-and-take between David and God is nothing short of remarkable. We can only imagine what it would be like for this to happen in one of our prayers. First, David addresses God with his complaint, and he suggests that God must intervene. Then God does! Immediately!

He says, "I will now arise. . . . I will protect them from those who malign them" (v. 5).

This is the first such incident among the Lament Psalms, but it is not the last. Also, we are not told exactly how this developed. Did God somehow audibly reply to David? Did He send an angel, as He did for Daniel in Daniel 9? All we know is that God told David, in response to his petition, that He would rise up and protect His people from those who malign them.

A grand truth arises from this psalm, and it is one that not only addresses David's present lament but also gives hope and encouragement to all of us who are reading over David's shoulder. In this psalm, God intervenes with clarity and forcefulness, which is a characteristic of the Laments. But the comment of David that follows God's promise of intervention is a soaring mountain of hopefulness for all of us.

David declares, "The words of the LORD are flawless, like silver purified in a crucible, like gold refined seven times" (v. 6). Hearing God's glorious promise of assistance leads David to remind his reader of the majestic, remarkable words of the Lord. We have God's flawless, refined, and purified words. To live the Psalms life is, in addition to realizing that God listens to our words and responds, to recognize that in God's words—provided in Scripture—we have His direct and inspired communication about His grand story!

Let's end our brief look at this psalm of lament by meditating on these final inspired words: "You, LORD, will keep the needy safe and will protect us forever from the wicked" (v. 7). He told us He would, and we have His flawless word on it.

Communal Lament 2: Psalm 79—
An Outcry of Despair over Loss

Those of us who live in a relatively safe nation—a country where Christians, while perhaps occasionally berated and disrespected, are not subject to much persecution—may not understand the intensity of this psalm of lament. Yet we can learn from Asaph's complaint some helpful lessons.

A quick reading of Psalm 79 will reveal a picture of the destruction God's people witnessed in their beloved homeland of Israel—namely, in their capital city of Jerusalem. We can skim over the details of that picture too easily if we don't make an effort to grasp the despair this would bring.

On a smaller scale—smaller because our country does not have God's specifically designed temple nor a divinely significant city such as Jerusalem as its base—think of the country in which you live enduring such a scenario.

Imagine the sorrow of seeing your capital attacked and destroyed. Of experiencing the loss of important buildings in that city. Of knowing that people were killed ruthlessly in the capital and that other countries in the region looked with reproach on your land.

Specifically, here is what Asaph observed.

- "The nations have invaded" (v. 1).
- "They have reduced Jerusalem to rubble" (v. 1).
- Servants and saints have died (v. 2).
- Blood has been shed in the city (v. 3).
- "We are objects of contempt to our neighbors" (v. 4).

Throughout history, people who have been subject to persecution and abuse at the hands of those who dislike Christianity have used the words of Psalm 79 to express their abject sadness.

In 1546, fourteen Christians who had chosen to separate from the established church in France were executed for their supposed crimes. As they faced their fiery death in Meaux, France, they sang the first verse of Psalm 79: "O God, the heathen are come into thine inheritance."

Ten years later, at Angiers, France, another martyr was burned to death for his faith. One historian records that as he died, he "continued to sing this Psalm till he . . . gave up his soul to God."

In London in the early seventeenth century, cruel and grizzly executions of one religious sect took place, mirroring the images of Psalm 79:2, and historians such as Luisa de Carvaja recorded the connection between the scene and the verses.

The point here is that the words Asaph recorded about his beloved land have been used in multiple places throughout history as martyrs have stood their ground and have seen in their impending death a connection with the destruction of Jerusalem.

The lamentable events Asaph detailed led him to a series of questions and statements that we—although not having suffered such great destruction—can ask in whatever troubling situations we find ourselves mired in. We too can sense a reason to cry out in situations in which we feel God could and perhaps should intervene, situations that bewilder us and make us wonder why He doesn't act.

For instance, Asaph wonders, "How long, LORD? Will you be angry forever?" (v. 5). Then he makes a suggestion to God: "Pour out your wrath on the nations that do not acknowledge you" (v. 6). And he says to the Lord, "Do not hold against us the sins of past generations; may your mercy come quickly to meet us" (v. 8).

These are understandable responses. But they might give us the wrong impression if we dwell only on them. These notes from Asaph sound as if they are people-centered—that they are requests we humans make because we can't stand the circumstances we are in and don't want to be troubled. While that may be partially true for all of us, we don't get the point of Asaph's comments until we get to verse 9. It is here that we begin to see how this lament—one that is hard to read because of the troubles it details—begins to spell out to us a singular truth that can guide us through our difficulties and help us see how to respond to lamentable situations.

Asaph says, "Help us, God our Savior, for the glory of your name."

In all circumstances of life—even the very hard ones—we can survive and endure if we seek God's glorification throughout.

Although God seemed angry with the nation of Israel for the sins and indiscretions of the people, their ultimate goal was their restoration for His glory.

And in the end, after all of God's dealings with both Israel and enemy nations—and even with us—we can come to the grand conclusion with which this passage ends: "We your people, the sheep of your pasture, will praise you forever; from generation to generation we will proclaim your praise" (v. 13).

If the Israelites, after seeing their nation destroyed and its holy temple demolished, can return praise to God, so can we. If the great martyrs of the faith can lean on this passage for hope as the fires of death arise, we too can use it to recount God's praise.

The Psalms life helps us understand real life by helping us realize that our circumstances, even those that feel uncomfortable, are given to us so we can proclaim God's goodness no matter what life brings our way.

Personal Lament 1: Psalm 13—
From Sighing to Singing

Have you ever noticed how close to each other are laughter and tears? You can see it especially in little children, who can be laughing about something when suddenly and inexplicably their happiness morphs into tears and sobbing.

This psalm of David moves the psalmist quickly from one to the other. In just six verses, he moves from mournful sadness to meaningful prayer to mountaintop rejoicing. This is the kind of personal lament we can all relate to, for when a difficulty clouds our focus and saddens our heart, how we long to return to joy!

The fact that we are turning from a big-picture problem of a communal lament (what is bigger than having your temple and capital city decimated?) to what might be considered a small-picture problem of a personal lament does not negate the reality of the pain being addressed.

David uses a repetitious lament-starter in the first two verses as he explains his situation. "How long?" he wonders about each of his complaints. This phrase is used several dozen times in the Old Testament, both by God and by His people. The Lord said to Moses, "How long will you refuse to keep my commands?" (Exodus 16:28). He also asked Moses, "How long will this wicked community grumble against me?" (Numbers 14:27). Elijah stood before the nation and asked, "How long will you waver between two opinions? If the LORD is God, follow him; but if Baal is God, follow him" (1 Kings 18:21).

Here David has four "How longs" for God.

- "How long, LORD? Will you forget me forever?" (v. 1).
- "How long will you hide your face from me?" (v. 1).

- "How long must I . . . have sorrow in my heart?" (v. 2).
- "How long will my enemy triumph over me?" (v. 2).

Forgotten by God. Unable to find God. Sorrow in the heart. Tired of enemies.

Does any of this sound even a little bit familiar? Of course it does. We have all been there in some way.

At times, there seems to be an impenetrable barrier between us and God. Those dry spells come because of troubling circumstances, and we are pretty sure we have been deleted from God's contact list. It's frightening to think we have to tackle life without our Father.

There are times when the only emotion we can conjure up is sadness. A loss too difficult to bear has drawn our heart into depression. Or a task too tough to complete has left us frustrated. Or perhaps a relationship too full of trouble has sucked the joy out of life.

And there are times when we seem to be surrounded by people who aren't exactly on our side, who tear down instead of build up or who criticize instead of encourage.

How long, we ask.

Part 2 of David's personal lament is to turn to God in specific prayer. Clearly, he was already praying through his "How long" list, but now, in verse 3, he gets precise.

He asks for the following from the Lord: a look and an answer, or put another way, "light to my eyes." He appeared to need understanding—perhaps an awareness of why he was struggling and what God had in store for him through his trials. His fear, he says to God, is that his enemies might overtake him and cause him to fall.

Help me, Lord, we plead along with the psalmist.

And then the song. At the end of the lament, as is the pattern, light returns to the troubled soul. After a time in God's presence, David emerges with confidence. His trust has been renewed because he recalls God's unfailing love. His heart leaps with newfound joy because he recognizes again the salvation God offers.

And he sings.

Think about those times when you have, while heavyhearted and beleaguered of spirit, dragged yourself to a Sunday morning worship service. You stand there surrounded by friends and family who begin to lift up their voices and perhaps even their hands in praise for God's greatness. And while they do, your lips move about as much as a ventriloquist's as you muse over how little you have to sing about.

Perhaps that is a perfect time to review David's personal gripe with God and remind yourself that you are a couple steps away from praise. You take a deep breath as others sing, you recall what it is you are troubled about, and you close your eyes in prayer, asking God, "Please look on me and answer."

It may take a while, but you could soon find yourself ready to tune up those pipes and sing along with others in praise as you recall that "[God] has been good to me" (v. 6).

The Psalms life sometimes calls for us to pause, review our situation, beg God for help, and rejoice when He reminds us what a good, good Father He really is.

Personal Lament 2: Psalm 142—About Giving Up

The lady should have given up. On government assistance and too poor to afford a computer to write the story in her head, she typed it on a typewriter and sent it off to a publisher. Over and over she went through the process of going to publishers with her book idea. And over and over she was rejected. But she persevered.

Finally, one publisher at a publishing house named Bloomsbury let his daughter read the manuscript, and she loved it.

For more than two decades, the book J. K. Rowling typed over and over again has been a mega-bestseller, and she became one of the richest women in the world by writing an entire series of Harry Potter books.

We love stories of people who refuse to give up.

David was one of those people. Psalm 142 is a lament that transforms into a testimony of turning to God when we feel like lying down and giving in to the enemies around us—whether poverty or people or problematic situations.

Again, we learn from the lament pattern, and we are reminded of the help we can gain from this way of intersecting our lives with our Father's love and protection.

David is in trouble. He is being chased down by King Saul, and he finds himself in a cave. From that darkened chamber, he cries out aloud to God, asking for mercy and clarifying his complaint.

The future king has grown weak in spirit as his enemies seek to trap him. In addition, he feels the anxiety of being alone in his crisis. "No one is concerned for me. I have no refuge," he declares (v. 4).

Perhaps you have never been trapped in a cave while a king and all of his henchmen traipse through the countryside looking for you. We can't really connect with that scenario.

But we can all recall those times when our spirit seemed depleted, when we sensed that those around us were not on our side, when we felt a bit alone in the world. You don't have to be a caveman to feel that way.

Perhaps those are the circumstances when we wonder if it's time to give up—to conclude that life is just too hard to navigate, and it's time to accept defeat.

That would be like J. K. Rowling throwing her manuscript into the English Channel instead of sending *Harry Potter and the Philosopher's Stone* to Bloomsbury, and never experiencing the joy of seeing her name on the front of a book (not to mention the gazillion dollars that would flow in).

David prayed a prayer of desperation instead of giving in to defeat. He turned his attention away from his cave and its potential for entrapment and death, and he cast his most heartfelt appeals to heaven.

"I cry to you, LORD," he said (v. 5). And he acknowledged his only hope.

"I say, 'You are my refuge,'" he blurted out (v. 5). And he recognized his only place of safety.

"I am in desperate need," he confessed (v. 6). And he gave up any pretense of self-confidence.

"Rescue me" (v. 6).

"Set me free" (v. 7).

Moments of deep despair that are turned into opportunities for ultimate trust are music to our Father's ears.

It is when we make our complaint, ignore the seeming comfort of giving up, and put ourselves into God's hands with hope and confidence that we can again find rescue. And when we do, we forget about giving up and we turn to praising God.

We find that around our cave of despair are those who will help, people who care about us. "The righteous will gather about me," said David, the newly rescued former cave-dweller, "because of your goodness to me" (v. 7).

There is no giving up in the real life. Sure, there are troubled moments and there are times when we feel alone, abandoned, and helpless.

But then we turn back to our God, acknowledge His power

as our rescuer, and allow Him to set us free from whatever has imprisoned us. Ahead may not be bestseller status and riches, but we know we will find reason again to praise God's name.

E i g h t

The Prayerful Life

You can *feel* the prayers in the book of Psalms.

These aren't "now I lay me down to sleep" prayers. These are painfully intense pleas from people who are laying their burdens at the feet of God. There is an urgency in their requests, a soaring eloquence in their praise, and a deep sorrow in their confession.

When was the last time you heard someone talk to God like this:

- "Answer me when I call to you" (4:1).
- "My soul is in deep anguish. How long, LORD, how long?" (6:3).
- "Have mercy and lift me up from the gates of death" (9:13).
- "Why, LORD, do you stand far off?" (10:1).
- "My God, my God, why have you forsaken me?" (22:1).

Prayers like these may seem a little foreign to us if we are accustomed to praying formula prayers that sometimes seem meant for people's ears instead of God's.

When Dwight Moody was preaching up a storm in nineteenth-century America, he called on a man to pray at one of his revival meetings. Apparently, the man got a little carried away with his prayer, and he went on and on and on. After a few minutes of his long-winded supplication, it became apparent that the man had no intention of stopping soon. Finally, Moody stood up and said, "While our brother is finishing his prayer, we are going to sing a hymn."

I wonder if this story would have had a different ending if the man had been praying like the psalmists!

We could never ignore any of the prayers recorded in the Psalms. Their power is too great, and their intensity is too real. And now we have those prayers at our disposal, to learn from and to use as examples when we feel the need for an intense prayer session with our Father.

What can we learn from these intense, pointed prayers? One lesson is that our prayers may need to diversify a little. I would surmise that for the most part, our prayers track along a pattern that looks something like this: We have a need, so we go to prayer. We know we should be thankful first, so we rush through a little "thanks for this beautiful day" sentence. Then we mention our petition: "Lord, please help my grandpa, who is having surgery." And we land the prayer with another quick thank-you and then the standard ending.

Do you think any of our formulaic prayers these days would have made it into the pages of sacred Scripture? Sure, it might seem like a silly question, but I have a reason for posing it. There is something unique and informative about the patterns we find in the psalms' petitions, and perhaps there is something in this collection that challenges our own pattern of prayer.

To help us find guidance in the prayers of the psalms, let's pull out three types of prayers: prayers of praise, prayers for assistance, and prayers for life issues. These various kinds of prayers can help us recharge our own conversations with God and remind us that our relationship is with a God who cares about the everyday stuff that comes our way.

As we examine these three types of prayers by looking at some Psalms that exemplify them, perhaps we will renew our communication with God and widen our appreciation for the many aspects of prayer.

Prayers of Praise

For two thousand years, the psalms have been a mainstay of Christian worship. From the first-century church through today, followers of Jesus have used many of the psalms as either a basis of worship (especially those traditions that use the Psalter) or as a complement to other worship songs that have been written more recently.

Therefore it makes sense to discuss the prayer psalms as tools we can use to help us lift our hearts in reverence and worship. We engage in the prayerful life—an essential aspect of the Psalms life—when we sing God's praises from the Psalms, for we are addressing God in adoration. And even when we are not singing those passages but instead reading them during our personal devotions, we are in a sense singing to our heavenly Father, to His beloved Son, and to the Spirit that indwells our hearts.

Let's take a brief look at one prayer psalm to discover how this kind of prayer can enhance our worship.

Psalm 103 lifts us to heights of glory from its very first words: "Praise the LORD, my soul" (v. 1). David proclaims the invigorating truth that it is his very soul that is called on to praise God, and indeed all of his inmost being. There is a completeness, an all-outness, to these words that plead with us to hold nothing back in our praise. That is what God's holy name deserves.

We continue in prayer and song by remembering—perhaps as the Israelites were called on to remember God's help in the desert—God's benefits.

- He forgives all our sins (v. 3).
- He heals all our diseases (v. 3).
- He redeems our life from the pit (v. 4).
- He crowns us with love and compassion (v. 4).
- He satisfies our desires with good things (v. 5).
- He restores our youth like the eagle's (v. 5).

No, we are not standing shoulder-to-shoulder with our fellow believers singing a great chorus of adoration as we read this Psalm in the comfort of our home, but our hearts can crescendo to those heights just the same. It is the words, and the truths behind them, that draw our hearts to God as we pray along with David.

David's prayer of praise reminds us as well of God's grand love for all people. It is through the Father's boundless care for the people He created that righteousness and justice can be introduced into the hearts of all. We send heartfelt praise heavenward when we realize that we are the oppressed—oppressed by sin—and we benefit from God's gracious gifts of righteousness and justice (v. 6). Our praise rises as we thank God for giving His righteousness to us through Christ and for allowing us to be justified through Jesus's sacrifice. How can we help but praise Him?

Let's look at some of the ways we can direct this praise song to God's glory.

- Praise God for His compassion and grace (v. 8).

- Praise God for His abounding love, which explains why He is slow to anger (v. 8).
- Praise God for His reticence to accuse, which speaks volumes about his forgiveness (v. 9).
- Praise God for His grace, which is the reason He does not treat us as we deserve (v. 10).
- Praise God for His great love (v. 11) and His forgiveness of our transgressions (v. 12).

We move along in this grand prayer and continue to sing God's glories, noting that He is our Father and our Creator. As our Father, He bestows undeserved compassion on us, which reminds us that He is indeed the Father of compassion (2 Corinthians 1:3). And as our Creator, He "knows how we are formed [and] remembers that we are dust" (Psalm 103:14), so He recognizes that we are frail in essence (vv. 15–16), especially compared with His omnipotence.

Yet in our frailty, this prayer reminds us, God's love is with us from eternity past until eternity future. We can never escape His love. He has special care for all of us who fear Him and obey His precepts (vv. 17–18).

And the praise is just beginning as the prayer psalm climbs to its mountain-peak ending. We sing of His kingdom and throne; we are reminded that God is surrounded by His messengers, the angels of heaven; and we think again about His mighty works in His dominion, which is the universe He created with just a word from His lips.

We need to return again and again to this song—this psalm of honor to the One who created all things, sustains all things, and calls all people everywhere to stand in holy awe of His greatness. It is a magnificent reminder of the many ways we can send praise God's way.

This prayer can become a cornerstone of the prayerful life as it continually calls us back to the reasons we stand and sing, "Praise the LORD, my soul, and forget not all his benefits" (v. 2).

Prayers for Assistance

As David wrote Psalm 3, he was in a heap of trouble.

His son Absalom was attempting to steal the throne from him. Absalom had been undermining David in Jerusalem for quite some time, and it appeared that he was on the verge of a major coup. He had taken a cadre of henchmen with him to Hebron, where he was going to declare himself Israel's new king. Absalom had a plan, and he had a following.

David had left town in fear, and he was in hiding again. When he said, "How many rise up against me!" (v. 1), he wasn't kidding. It seemed that with the people against him and with his son leading the charge, his days as king were numbered.

He needed deliverance in the same way we need salvation. Without God's intervention in either of our cases, we are doomed to defeat. So, seeking redemption, David cried out to God in all sincerity. He cried out to the Lord for assistance.

He cried out for the security we spoke of in chapter 6, for he said, "You, LORD, are a shield around me" (v. 3). And look at what happened.

- Glory was bestowed on him (v. 3).
- His head was lifted high (v. 3).
- God answered him (v. 4).
- He could rest, finally. He had been on the run, but now he could relax in God's arms (v. 5).
- He left fear behind him (v. 6).

David wasn't the only psalmist who cried out for help. In Psalm 42, we read the pleas of the Sons of Korah as they petition God for help, with a feeling we all deal with from time to time: being downcast.

How many times has someone said to you, "What's going on with you? You seem a little down today."

Of course, as we normally do, we shrug it off or make up a quick excuse. "Oh, I'm fine. I'm just thinking about a big project I have to do."

Often we don't want to talk to people about what has us down, because we don't want to be vulnerable. Yet here is an open invitation to place our problems, no matter what the origin, at God's feet.

This is one of those passages that gives us both the problem and the solution. It's as if the psalmist were having a bit of a discussion with himself about a serious subject, and he is enough aware of his relationship with God to provide both the negative side and the positive.

I'll leave it up to psychologists and counselors to decide whether this is the best way of dealing with life's difficulties, but it does seem to be working in this psalm.

The troubled one asks himself, "Why . . . are you downcast? Why so disturbed within me?" (v. 5).

And then, a God-directed answer: "Put your hope in God, for I will yet praise him" (v. 5).

Verse 6 continues with a similar two-part prayer: "My soul is downcast," followed by "I will remember you from the land of the Jordan."

The One who led the people into the land and gave them exactly what He promised He would give them is the One who can lift the downcast heart and allow His help to sweep over the psalmist (v. 7).

Prayers for Life Issues

A bad past (Psalm 25:6–10). We covered David's big-time sins earlier, but his cries for help seem to be the prayers of someone who cannot get spiritual freedom from earlier, more youthful sins. Of course, we all have a bad past in the sense that we got started sinning when we were just children. But for some, the recollection of youthful foolishness is stifling.

The psalmist prays, "Remember, LORD, your great mercy and love, for they are from of old" (v. 6). By contrast, he asks God to forget "the sins of my youth and my rebellious ways" (v. 7).

Have you ever had a conversation with someone you went to school with as a kid, and before you know it, you hear this: "Hey, remember the time you . . . ," and they bring up an incident you regret to this day? Something that got you into major trouble with your parents or teachers or maybe even a police officer. You cringe, because just the reminder of the incident is embarrassing, and you wish everyone could just forget it.

God can do just that. He will not hold our youthful indiscretions over us once we confess them in Jesus's name. What a grand thing it is to say with David, "Guard my life and rescue me; do not let me be put to shame, for I take refuge in you. May integrity and uprightness protect me, because my hope, LORD, is in you" (vv. 20–21).

A bad past is safe in God's hands. What hope and joy that can give us!

Worthless things (Psalm 101:1–4). If we were to make a list of things that we might consider "vile and vulgar" (v. 3 NLT) or "worthless" (ESV), it would be rather long. We won't go through that exercise here, because we all know which worthless things trip us up; we don't need any assistance in that category.

What can we learn about how to handle sinful items that come before our eyes? David starts this extremely helpful, practical psalm with praise. There's a pretty good hint right there, because how incongruous would it be for us to entertain ourselves with worthless things while God's praises were leaving our lips! So we sing praise as a way to avoid worthless things.

Notice how David describes the life of one who praises and does not get distracted by sin: "blameless" (v. 2). We've seen this word before, in an earlier chapter, and it is just as useful here. In general terms ("I will be careful to lead a blameless life") and in specific terms ("I will conduct the affairs of my house with a blameless heart"), this prayer shows the way (v. 2).

It's a prayer with both a praise to God and a commitment to careful living.

And it is a great precursor to the question that arises in Psalm 119: "How can a young person stay on the path of purity?" (v. 9). That passage also includes a prayer of praise (v. 12) and a commitment (vv. 10–11), and then it adds this valuable third element to the formula for avoiding worthless activities: "living according to [God's] word" (v. 9).

The prayer of Psalm 101:1–4 helps all believers establish some fence posts around the perimeter of their lives—guides that will keep us within God's will and help us to "have nothing to do with what is evil" (v. 4).

Great reversals (Psalm 30). It's not unusual to hear young Christian couples who are just starting out their married lives tell of times they struggled financially. It's the rare young man and wife who don't wonder how they are going to pay their bills as they finish school or work at entry-level jobs. Yet it is also not unusual to hear stories about young couples who didn't know how they were going to pay a bill, until an envelope mysteriously appeared in their mailbox with just the right amount of money.

This happened on one occasion to Sue and me when we were a poor married college couple.

Psalm 30 suggests that there are times when God provides for us at just the right time and in just the right circumstance, and David here prays a prayer of thanks for situations like that. Let's look at some of them.

- Gloating enemies are silenced (v. 1).
- Illness is turned into wellness (vv. 2–3).
- Weeping is changed into rejoicing (v. 5).
- Wailing is turned into dancing (v. 11).
- Sadness is changed into joy (v. 11).

Great reversals deserve great praise, and the psalmist gives us a number of examples. When we see God work in our lives, rescuing us from what might have been and guiding us to the life He desires for us, we can say,

- "I will exalt you, Lord" (v. 1).
- "Sing the praises of the Lord, you his faithful people" (v. 4).
- "My heart [will] sing your praises and not be silent. Lord my God, I will praise you forever" (v. 12).

The prayers of the psalms cover the gamut of life's experiences. They encourage us with their realism, and they wow us with their revelation of God's greatness. As we continue to seek God's guidance for living the Psalms life, one practical thing we can do is to keep exploring the prayers in these 150 chapters. Our study of them will never be exhausted, for they will never stop inspiring us and lifting us toward our gracious heavenly Father.

Nine

The Sanctuary Life

L et me tell you about one of the best people I know.
I have admired this man for many years, first as a fellow board member at the Christian school our kids went to and later as a missionary supported by our church. I'll not name him, because I know he would not want the attention.

I know him as a man of faith and a true servant of our Lord. He had a successful pastorate before he felt God calling his family to serve in a nation halfway around the world.

During their long tenure in a faraway land, my friend and his wife endured a number of serious setbacks—both health problems and the normal difficulties of serving in a developing country with a questionable infrastructure. By the end of their time on the mission field, they had moved into a tiny apartment without even a full kitchen. One of the reasons they did that was so they could help finance the schooling for students at the seminary where they taught. Every single day of their existence while overseas was a struggle financially and physically. Yet they journeyed on without complaint.

Finally, it came time for them to retire. They were looking forward to coming home to their small house and getting a break from their rigorous routine.

So what happened as soon as they returned home? An unprecedented flood hit their city, filling their basement and taking out both their furnace and their water heater.

And still I heard no complaints, only requests for prayer.

Here were two well-educated, talented people who knew how to communicate, teach, and encourage others. They had skills that could have served them well had they sought financial gain and an easy lifestyle. Yet even in retirement, they faced money problems and little security.

Good people. Dedicated followers of God.

Struggling.

This shouldn't happen, we often think. Why should God's people struggle while ungodly people thumb their nose at Him, rake in huge salaries, and vacation in Aruba?

If you find yourself asking those kinds of questions, you are not alone. While I have no evidence that my friends ask them, I know of a man who did. And he was no slouch in the talent department either. Like my friend's wife, he was a music teacher, and he helped lead the singing at a pretty prestigious institution: the temple in Israel.

Asaph's struggle was not too different from one that most of us, as people of God, might experience. He looked around at other people in his larger circle of friends and acquaintances, and he saw something that troubled him greatly. He noticed that some folks who had nothing to do with God were finding success in ways he simply could not duplicate.

Perhaps his ungodly neighbor, who was not so nice to his wife and got drunk on weekends, had invested in the Jerusalem stock market and had struck it rich. Meanwhile, Asaph, who trusted God with his finances, had invested in a camel rental company that went belly up.

Or maybe another friend down at the office who never darkened the gate of the temple always seemed to be bragging about the latest model of chariot that was parked securely in his garage at home, while Asaph's beat-up old buggy was perpetually in the shop.

Silly speculation aside, here is what Asaph said in Psalm 73: "I envied the arrogant when I saw the prosperity of the wicked" (v. 3). As he watched this happening all around him, Asaph says, he nearly lost his religion! "My feet had almost slipped; I had nearly lost my foothold" (v. 2).

This is real life, for my friend today and for Asaph so long ago.

And for us.

This is how things roll sometimes, and it really messes with our minds. We start to look over at the people in nearby cubicles, and we say with Asaph, "They have no struggles" (v. 4); "they are free from common human burdens" (v. 5). We move through verses 4 through 12, and we sound an amen at Asaph's every new complaint.

"And they don't even love God!" we mutter.

Then, after adding it all up in our heads, we might conclude, as Asaph does in verse 13, "Surely in vain I have kept my heart pure." We figure that our sanctified life—our dedication to holiness and to godliness—has been a gargantuan waste of time. After all, the people who are getting ahead in life wouldn't know holiness from a hole in one, and they're the ones who are winning!

We fret (v. 14). We feel oppressed (v. 16).

And we cheer Asaph on as he says, in effect, "Why not cash this all in and live like everybody else?"

His story begins to sound like one of those Facebook postings that drags you in with its tantalizing headline: "Asaph Plans to Give Up on God: You Won't Believe What He Said in His Prayer."

But as you click through the "read more" section, you find a surprise.

You discover that this is not the story of another believer who has dropped out of the faith because of his circumstances. You find that it is a believer who has been restored because of God's help. This becomes the part of the story you really wanted to find, because you have wondered aloud at times about the same questions Asaph had.

You hoped and prayed that there was a positive solution. And at verse 17, you found it.

You begin to see that Asaph's conflict reveals to us that there is a solution to our angst. There is a cure for our disappointment. There is a salve for our wounded spirit.

And it involves a mysterious thing called "sanctuary"!

Asaph struggled mightily until, as he reports, "I entered the sanctuary of God" (v. 17).

When Asaph went into God's sanctuary and lifted his eyes and his spirit toward Him in awe and adoration, everything came into proper focus.

- It wasn't because he encountered a really with-it praise team banging out another remarkable Chris Tomlin hit.
- It wasn't because the preacher was cool-in-jeans-and-untucked-shirt amazing, telling stories fascinating enough to make the people forget their lattes.
- It had nothing to do with other people—which is astounding, because the problems in Asaph's mind were all about other people!

In the Lord's sanctuary, Asaph could suddenly see life from a different perspective—God's. He could begin to understand that even if everything makes the ungodly look like the most fortunate people on earth, there is a much better way to think about the situation.

When Asaph stepped into the sanctuary, he began to realize that everyone who seemed to be having success without God was existing in a short-lived fantasy with a horrible ending. Despite the sports car in the driveway, the burgeoning bank account, the million-mile airline card, and the carefree lifestyle, they were in dire trouble.

They were like the guy in the TV commercial who is lazily cutting his lawn with his riding mower in front of his mansion of a house. He looks for all the world like he is rolling in riches, until he turns to the camera and reveals the sorry truth: "I'm up to my eyeballs in debt!"

When Asaph entered God's sanctuary, he began to understand for the first time that the people who seemed to have it so good were really on slippery ground (v. 18). They were destined for failure (v. 19). They were up to their eyeballs in trouble.

While in the sanctuary of God—where we all need to go when we wonder what He is doing and how we can get in touch with Him to find out about life—Asaph discovered that worrying about others is a poor substitute for worshiping God. He was reminded of God's caring protection (v. 23), God's guidance (v. 24), God's strength (v. 26), and the safety of trusting God's sovereignty (v. 28).

Who of us has not been troubled by comparing our failures with the apparent success of people in our circle of friends and family? We can't help but agree sometimes with Asaph's observations in the early part of Psalm 73.

But it doesn't do us any good to stay there. If we find it

comfortable to remain in gripe mode, we allow ourselves to get stuck in our self-created malaise. We cancel out any hope of finding help. That is why we must break free from our worries about others and go to God—enter His sanctuary—and listen to His all-surpassing wisdom.

How, then, do we apply the principle of the sanctuary, the place that turned it all around for Asaph? In his day, of course, the normal context for the word *sanctuary* was the temple, the place of worship for the people of Israel. But what Asaph needed was not merely a place of worship. He needed to refocus his attention from the world around him to the God above him, so he could learn— so he could gain an understanding about an important topic that troubled him. He needed to be in God's presence.

In those days, that reality could be experienced in a way we can't experience it today. That was because within the temple walls *was* the presence of God—both realized in the holy of holies and symbolized by the ark of the covenant.

Asaph needed to go to a place where the world would not intrude in his fellowship with the Father and where God's still, small voice could be heard. In this case, it was where he could realize—contrary to his own feelings—that the fruit of the wicked is ruin and that the ultimate result of godliness is the smile of God's blessing.

Matthew Henry, in his classic commentary, explained the sanctuary in a way that may sound a bit dated but still makes great sense today: "The sanctuary must be the resort of the tempted soul."[1] Indeed, Asaph was tempted to turn away from truth, and he needed to get into God's presence to listen to His wisdom and reject the foolishness of his own tormented thinking.

So, since we don't have a holy of holies in our church auditorium, how do we find this sanctuary? Is it possible to sense that presence today? Where do we go when the troubles of daily existence in a fallen world make us feel like our feet are slipping?

Nowhere.

Think of all those movies you have seen in which a character is struggling mightily with some kind of life-changing problem. Often, it seems, it is a person who has committed a crime, and he doesn't know where to turn for help. So he walks into a church, sits somewhere near the back, and is in one way or another influenced by the surroundings to make his next move.

This is a stereotypical approach to getting help from God, and it might even seem to align well with Psalm 73.

The solution Asaph found, however, is not about a physical place, although such a setting did offer some assistance. It is about finding God himself—His *presence*—to be a sanctuary. We are not sure what caused this reality to dawn on Asaph, but for some reason he suddenly knew that going into God's sanctuary would reveal the answer he needed.

If the answer is truly found in going not into a place but into a presence, we are indeed fortunate. Believers in Jesus Christ have access to the sanctuary of God's presence at all times. He is the Holy Spirit, living in our inner being. Could it be that a reminder of His indwelling might be a revelation to us in the same sense that entering the temple was a life-changing revelation for Asaph?

Longtime pastor and author Ray Stedman put it in these terms: "God lives in us. To draw near to Him is to enter the sanctuary. We enter the sanctuary in various ways: by exposing ourselves to His truth in the Scripture; or by facing truth we have forgotten as we fellowship with other Christians; or by directly praying to God and changing our thinking from natural to spiritual."[2]

Whenever we find ourselves confused about life and our place in this world, our best move is toward God—calling on the Holy Spirit to give us the insight and guidance He alone can provide.

So what other insights did Asaph discover on this hallowed ground in God's sanctuary?

• *Being held by God's hand.* Is there anything more calmly comforting than a held hand? Whenever I am guiding one of my younger grandchildren along during one of our adventures, I love reaching down to grasp that tiny hand, hoping to provide security for that little one. Whenever Sue and I are taking a walk, two hands grasped together speak volumes about a long-standing relationship that never grows old. And who can forget the Beatles' reminder of young love, "I Want to Hold Your Hand"?

Asaph proclaimed, "I am always with you; you hold me by my right hand" (v. 23). In the sanctuary, he discovered that something special happens—something beyond the comfort of a touch—when God is at our right hand. In Psalm 16:8, David says, "I keep my eyes always on the Lord. With him at my right hand, I will not be shaken." Bible scholar Derek Kidner says that this posture signifies "a person who will stand by one."[3]

In God's presence, Asaph discovers not only the slippery slope on which the ungodly stand but also the comfort and security of having our eternal Father stand beside us, holding our hand. The sanctuary life takes on a warm, personal touch for Asaph, and for us.

• *Being guided by God's counsel.* Have you ever had someone important take you into his or her counsel? I try to counsel the teenagers I am privileged to interact with through the high school where my daughter teaches. Each year for more than a decade, I was able to travel with a group of teens on mission trips to three countries and Alaska. And there I would try to establish a relationship with them so I could provide Christian counsel.

Interestingly, some do not accept this counsel, for they do not allow me into their world for whatever reason. But others willingly talk to me about their life, and I can walk them through Christian life situations and provide cautions, knowledge, and direction.

Are we like that with God? Some of us don't really want Him intruding into our lives, so we keep Him at arm's length, rejecting the opportunity to learn from Him. Asaph apparently took advantage of this opportunity to learn and grow: "You guide me with your counsel" (Psalm 73:24).

In God's sanctuary, after He changes our perspective and holds our hand, He gives us perfect guidance for our life ahead. What we do with His guidance dictates our growth in Him or our lack of it.

So add matchless counsel to the advantages of the sanctuary life.

• *Seeing God as our greatest desire.* Outside of the sanctuary of God's presence—probably where we live most of our life—we are distracted by so many things.

We are so much like the dog in *Up*, it's not even funny. Dug is his name, and he can talk. When he does, he explains to the older man, Carl, that his master has given him the capability of talking. But then, right in the middle of this great revelation, Dug becomes completely distracted and shouts, "Squirrel!" The scene has become an iconic representation of people who can't stick to one thing without getting sidetracked.

Sound familiar? We go through our days being pulled aside by so many different attractions that it is hard to focus on just one thing. We really want to stick to what is important, whether it is work or family or even our relationship with God. But just as we get settled in and begin to concentrate on, let's say reading the Bible—"Squirrel!"

Asaph discovered, in his visit to the sanctuary, that there is but one great desire, and that is the Lord. He concluded, "Earth has nothing I desire besides you" (v. 25).

Can we say that?

We enjoy being told that the wicked will get their comeuppance. We are comforted by the thought of God's presence. But this one scares us a little. It stands for commitment, for clarity of purpose, and for focus on God and His desires for us in this world.

Notice, though, that what comes next in this passage helps us to stop being distracted and to start fixing our desires on God.

• *Accessing God's strength.* Do you recall what Jesus, just before He ascended to heaven, told the disciples they would receive? We normally answer that question by saying that He told them they would receive the Holy Spirit. But the first thing He told them they would receive is power. He said, "You will receive power when the Holy Spirit comes on you" (Acts 1:8).

In 1 Corinthians 2:4, Paul explained that despite his own personal weakness, he came to the people of Corinth with a message and with preaching that were both "a demonstration of the Spirit's power."

We have power from God, through the Holy Spirit, to overcome many of our weaknesses. For instance, if one weakness is "Squirrel!"—the inability to keep our mind on the things of God—the power of the Holy Spirit is available to help us gain the focus we need.

As is true of many of the psalms, the ending of Psalm 73 is so much more fulfilling and encouraging than the beginning. Asaph began well back in verse 1 with a quick word about God's goodness, but he suddenly transitioned to his long complaint.

We tag along with him, agreeing with his objections and thinking of the grievances we could add to them if we ever had the chance to enter our comments into Holy Writ.

And then there is that surprising switch that so often happens in a psalm. Complaints suddenly turn into pathways to satisfying solutions, and we pick up speed as we run through the psalmist's uplifting collection of happy revelations about God's goodness to us.

In Psalm 73, those positive changes build to an exciting conclusion, one that challenges us to try to replicate Asaph's triumphant transformation. We look at his final verse, and we discover that in it we have a motto—possibly a meme to put on Facebook, but more importantly, a crescendo of hopefulness and resolution.

May we discover in the sanctuary life the courage and strength to say with Asaph, "As for me, it is good to be near God. I have made the Sovereign LORD my refuge" (v. 28).

That conclusion reminds us that a trip to the sanctuary of God is an excursion we all need to take.

Ten

The Content Life

Social media can make the content life a challenge.

Think about it. Log on to your Facebook account, and you will be bombarded by a never-ending stream of the amazing things your "friends" are doing.

- Katie posts more pix of those incredible meals she cooks, which you view as you enjoy your third straight day of Taco Bell's finest munchies.
- Cheryl displays her kids in their baseball uniforms, holding a growing collection of trophies her little MVPs have won. And they are still in elementary school!
- Mike's photo montage of the majestic bookshelf he built reminds you that you've been subscribing to a handyman magazine for ten years and still can't make a decent miter cut.
- Meanwhile, your friend Keith is posting photos from another NBA game. How can he afford the tickets and the time?
- Scott and his wife are in Europe. Again. Don't they ever work?

- Paula created a meme with an fresh, beautiful way to explain God's love.
- Melinda just got a new dog, and even though it is a golden retriever pup that looks just like every other golden retriever pup you've ever seen, she has 735 likes.
- And every mother you know has another picture of her too-cute-for-words baby doing some new smile-producing activity.

And on and on it goes. You wipe the hot sauce off your face, crumple up your taco wrapper, and go back to trying to squeeze enough money out of your budget to replace the sliding glass door that just fell off its track when you went outside to figure out why the deck is leaning that way again.

You know nobody wants to see *that* on Facebook.

We want to be content, we know we are supposed to be content, and we resolve to be happy with the situation God has placed us in, but we sometimes struggle with being satisfied with life. We are even happy for our friends who seem to have at least the Facebook part of their lives together, yet we sigh the sigh of discontentment.

I would venture a guess that if I were your friend and I was in your living room talking about this with you, you would roll your eyes if I were to suggest that one solution to your lack of contentment is found in Psalm 23. Oh, I know you wouldn't do that out of disrespect. After all, you know Psalm 23 is just as inspired as John 3:16, and you count it one of your favorite Bible passages.

It's just that you might think, "Here we go again." You could probably quote portions of this famous chapter, and you've surely heard great messages on it. You'd probably point to that budget you are trying to wrestle into shape and tell me you don't understand how David's words from thousands of years ago could really help lift your spirits and lead to a life of contentment.

To that I would ask your indulgence to allow me to explain Psalm 23 from a perspective you may not have considered: a perspective of brokenness. I might not be able to help you get past the idea that Melinda's dog is way cuter than yours, that Scott's vacations are more exotic than your weekend getaways at Motel 6, and that Mike could build a storage shed out of toothpicks if he wanted to—in other words, I may not find in Psalm 23 justifications for life's inequities—but I can tell you that this chapter has helped me battle through life's greatest tragedy in my search to reconnect with contentment, and it may help you find the reality of God's greatness and love in whatever situation you are facing.

A perspective from brokenness—a bottom-up approach—is surely better than a perspective of looking through your friend's rose-colored glasses—a top-down approach.

Earlier in this book, I mentioned the night our family's life was shattered to pieces. I told about having my heart ripped open and my soul devastated by the sudden, unexpected, and unbearable death of our beautiful seventeen-year-old daughter Melissa.

I will never get over this loss. It haunts me every day and in a multitude of ways. The pain of not ever seeing her, hearing her, laughing with her, even simply parenting her, is agonizing and never ending. The disheartening reality of not seeing her graduate, go to college, get married, and present us with grandkids—as her sisters have done—is almost too much to contemplate.

In one sense, knowing that my baby girl is lying in a grave just a few miles from our home sears my inner being every time I think about it.

Yet there is something about Psalm 23 that has soothed my soul and allowed me to rediscover contentment in our new life despite the horror that is losing a child. I am not sure if it is the grand eloquence of David's words so carefully crafted in the Hebrew and so meticulously and beautifully translated into English. I am not sure if it is the wonderful imagery. I am not sure if it is the godly truth. It may be a combination of these elements that has come alongside me to provide solace, hope, understanding, and insight that helps me go on despite the weight of my sorrow.

Perhaps as I share how Psalm 23 has helped me extract contentment out of pain, you can make it a key component of living the Psalms life for yourself and your family. Perhaps you'll sense that a passage with the power to keep a grieving father going can help you too find true contentment in the struggles that populate your life. Perhaps the contentment in these six timeless verses can spill over into your heart and fill your mind as you ask God's guidance in your search for the quiet confidence of a satisfying existence.

Let's see what Psalm 23 provides that can help us settle into the content life.

To Be Content, I Need Redirection
"The LORD is my shepherd" (Psalm 23:1).

In the toughest season of our family's life, the help we needed was not necessarily the kind a shepherd is noted for. We didn't need a shepherd who would leave his flocks and go look for a missing sheep; we weren't wandering off. In fact, we knew where our lost sheep was: Melissa is in heaven. We didn't need a brave shepherd who would protect us from predators. We were surrounded by friends and family. But what we did need was a shepherd who would guide us from one field to another.

Sometimes shepherds need to do that. They will see that the field where the sheep have been grazing for a while is no longer sufficient. The food supply has been depleted or there's no water. So they gently redirect the sheep to a new location—a place that will meet their needs. They guide them to a place more suited to their ongoing sustenance.

We needed that kind of assistance in the aftermath of Melissa's untimely death. In the field we had grown accustomed to, life had been moving along in a normal fashion. Our two oldest girls had graduated from college. One was married, and the other was off soon to her first teaching job. Melissa and her brother Steve were moving through high school at an acceptable pace. Faith, family, and school was our field, and the grazing was good.

Then came tragedy, and everything was disrupted. We could no longer stay where we were; life demanded a change. We needed guidance to know how to move into a new, foreign situation. We had to have the Shepherd's help in knowing how to think, how to live, how to survive grief, and how to negotiate what seemed like a million other new aspects of our existence in a different place.

Surrounded by grief and surprising new questions about life and faith, I needed the Shepherd to direct my steps, redirect my thoughts, and inform my understanding of God's interaction in this new life we were forced to live.

Allow me to give an example of how my Shepherd assisted me. In the old field, where I had been my whole life, my faith was marked by doubt-free acceptance of God's role. Never once did I spend time wondering if what I had been taught growing up about the Christian faith or had learned at my Christian college and our Bible-teaching churches or had discovered on my own should be questioned. My faith was real, true, and trustworthy. It was solid ground.

But something changed when Melissa didn't come home that night in June and four days later we watched through tear-clouded eyes and with trembling hearts as her body was lowered into a grave.

Suddenly I had to rethink everything. I had to decide if what I had always believed was really true. If this was the reward for a lifetime of faith, could Christianity be a mirage? I needed to be reassured that God was sovereign, that His love was genuine, and that the gospel was as real after Melissa died as it was before. I needed a Shepherd to guide me to a new field of thinking.

As I examined this idea, and as I tried to think deeply about what faith meant to me, I felt as if the Shepherd helped me make some hard decisions.

To begin with, I had to think about whether this matter of faith—and God's plan for salvation as spelled out in the Bible— was indeed just about me. Was it just about Melissa?

I had to look at the whole story of Scripture—from the beginning in the garden of Eden and Adam's sin, through the Old Testament stories of the Jewish people, through the story of Jesus's birth in Matthew and Luke, through His death, burial, and resurrection in the Gospels—and decide: was Melissa, was our family, the center of this story?

Is the Bible narrative, which culminates in the gospel message, about Dave Branon's family? Was my daughter's tragic death the centerpiece of the story, and did that story no longer work because Melissa died?

Many people think this way, and I wondered if they might be right. Was I wasting my time with this thing called Christianity because it did not stop me from losing my daughter? And because this bad thing happened to me, did that give me the right to say the whole story doesn't work, as if I were the centerpiece of it all?

A couple of verses in the Old Testament gave me insight into this as I sought the Shepherd's help. Both verses are in the Psalms. Psalm 116:15 says, "Precious in the sight of the LORD is the death of his faithful servants." And the second verse is Psalm 139:16—a verse we examined earlier: "All the days ordained for me were written in your book before one of them came to be."

These two verses helped open up a grand reality for me and usher me into the new field I now occupy.

I began to sense, as my Shepherd informed my thinking, that in Melissa's case, God's plan of salvation—which is the story of the entire Bible—worked exactly as God designed it.

On the day Melissa died, God was not surprised to find her entering heaven. Her life story had already been written, and God in His sovereignty knew it was complete. Although we did not know that morning when she left home to take her final exams of her junior year of high school that her story had just seventeen years, ten months, and fifteen days in it, God did. Her death did not destroy the gospel; *it celebrated the gospel.* Because Melissa was a child of God through faith in Jesus's death, burial, and resurrection, God was waiting expectantly with open arms to receive his precious saint on June 6, 2002.

Her death was not a mistake. It was part of God's grand plan. And He celebrated her homecoming on that day. Melissa's death did not mean God's plan had failed. It meant that it worked!

God received the glory that day because His plan worked to perfection and another faithful servant was successfully welcomed into heaven.

Having said all of that, I can tell you that this does not make me any less sad. It does not mean that I am okay with never being able to talk to her on this earth again. It doesn't mean our family does not miss her every single day and that we are not incredibly saddened by her death. It does not mean that I am typing these words without tears, for they are surely falling still!

None of that goes away. But the reality of Melissa's salvation and her presence with God in heaven allows me to keep my faith, because it is not about me. It is about God and His eternal glory.

Scripture tells us that we can have hope in the face of death. We can mourn in a way that is not like the hopeless sorrow of those without faith.

The Lord, my shepherd, changed my thinking and led me to a new field—a new normal in life that allows me to continue trusting Him and living for Him, and gives me a fresh hope of seeing my Melissa again.

To Be Content, I Need Satisfaction and Solace
"I lack nothing. He makes me lie down in green pastures, he leads me beside quiet waters" (Psalm 23:1–2).

I am going to beg your indulgence on this part of the great psalm of contentment. Would it be okay with you if I quote myself briefly? I have thought through this topic already in my book *Beyond the Valley*, so I have already explained what I've learned from the "I lack nothing" part of Psalm 23 as clearly as I can. Here's what I said in that book.

> Our unavoidable tendency to want what we cannot have causes me to rethink this promise—to discover the connection between the Shepherd, the green pastures, and the still waters. Intrinsic in the character of the Shepherd is something that is supposed to make me not desire the unattainable. Because the Lord is the Shepherd, there is expected to be something in Him that relieves the heart from the pain of expectations.
>
> What is it? What about God as Shepherd can erase my wants even though all of my being tells me that I cannot

be satisfied? What God-characteristics or God-actions will flip the switch on my inner-being's got-to-have-it mechanism to stop it from the painful pursuit of the impossible?

In one sense, I cannot want for my daughter any more than what she has. In a sense, she has more than I could ever give her. She knows of a joy and peace that a father can only dream of for his daughter. For her, I cannot possibly want anything greater.

In a sense, I have given up my daughter so she could have ultimate joy and happiness. I don't have to want for her anymore. For that, I must give up my want—I must sacrifice my desire.

That is an unspeakable satisfaction and a sure solace in the midst of sorrow. Somehow, even in the middle of our pain, God understands and cares for our wants and gives us green pastures of contentment and still waters of hope.

To Be Content, I Need Restoration and Direction
"He refreshes my soul. He guides me along
the right paths" (Psalm 23:3).

I've never restored an older car to mint condition, but it sure sounds like fun. My car of choice would be a 1967 Camaro. My brother bought a brand-new version of this car when I was a kid, and I have always thought it would be cool to have one just like his, restored to the condition his was in when he drove it off the lot.

What I am pretty sure I'll never be able to do with the car of my dreams I have done for myself, and so can you. At one time in our lives, we were made new when we trusted Jesus Christ as Savior.

But along the way, sin dings us up and trouble clogs up our engine a bit. We lose that new-Christian smell, and we start to look a little like my fourteen-year-old Hyundai.

We need restoration.

As I was looking through Melissa's Bible one day, I came upon a passage that she had marked by circling the first verse number and drawing a smiley face in the margin. I thought it was an odd passage to flag with such a happy symbol, but as I think about restoration of our souls, it almost takes my breath away.

Here is what the passage says: "We . . . glory in our sufferings, because we know that suffering produces perseverance; perseverance, character; and character, hope" (Romans 5:3–4). In this passage, Paul gives us the details about how God restores our soul after we go through a time of suffering. Of course, Melissa didn't know the extent to which her dad would need this reminder, but the steps of restoration can't be any clearer.

Suffering produces perseverance—the quality of not giving up or giving in when we are troubled.

Perseverance builds character—a quality by which we are able to use our suffering to help and guide others.

Character leads to hope—that quality we so desperately need after we pick ourselves up from whatever causes us to suffer. We need hope, which is not a pretend "I hope my team wins" thing but a real, solid "because of God's love, we have victory in life" kind of thing.

Indeed, God restores our soul like nothing else in this world can.

We need that restoration because it reestablishes our relationship with God and moves us back into effectiveness as Christ's representatives in the world. Psalm 19:7 reminds us: "The law of the LORD is perfect, refreshing the soul."

If I were ever to pick up a fixer-upper 1967 Camaro with designs on bringing it back to glory, I would need help. I would need to find a lot of YouTube videos on how to take a car apart in preparation for restoring it. I would need the repair manual for the car so I would know how to put it back together. In other words, I would need a source to guide me.

That's what Psalm 19:7 and Melissa's smiley face passage Romans 5:3–4 give us in terms of reviving our soul and putting it back into showroom condition. We would be lost in our effort at renewal without the clear teaching of God's Word.

To Be Content, I Need Protection and Comfort
"Even though . . . your rod and your staff,
they comfort me" (Psalm 23:4).

Have you ever been really frightened? Perhaps you've had to be in an unsafe part of town at night, and you weren't sure how to reach a safe area. Maybe you were at home alone, and you were certain you heard someone in the basement. You were so scared, you couldn't even remember the number for 911. Or perhaps you were taking a walk, and someone's Doberman came charging toward you, barking, with his teeth bared.

If you were ever in a frightened state like that, you were not content. You were not satisfied and relaxed. You were not happy with the situation in a way that made your heart calm and gave your soul peace.

You needed protection!

You needed a policeman to show up or the dog owner to call off his pooch.

We need God's protection in so many of life's circumstances.

In Psalm 23:4, David suggests a scenario that shows us what true danger looks like. David talks about walking through the valley of darkness. Indeed, "darkest valley" is properly translated "valley of the shadow of death" in many Bibles, but it is that and other possibilities. Death is the worst circumstance this verse could address, but it is not limited to that. The valley of darkness could suggest the many other life situations where we find ourselves in fear.

Whenever we are standing face-to-face with something we fear, we can think of our Shepherd, who possesses two items that represent His care for us: His rod and His staff. Those two things reassure David because they signify both God's protection (the rod, with which a shepherd fended off wild animals) and His comfort (the staff, with which a shepherd would keep the flock together).

To Be Content, I Need Provision and Anointing
"You prepare a table. . . . You anoint my head
with oil" (Psalm 23:5).

The crisis has passed. The threat has been thwarted by the Shepherd, who wielded His rod against the intruding problem and surrounded you with the comforting crook of His staff.

And now it is time to celebrate.

At times, it seems impossible to celebrate after trouble has hit or tragedy has covered us with sorrow. It is easy, when we have faced difficulties, to fall into a pattern of melancholy, afraid of the next problem and weighed down with a sadness that only reluctantly releases its grip on us.

This many years after getting that heart-wrenching phone call telling me my daughter was gone, I can still easily slip into a deep sadness. Tears seem always waiting to fall when I recall what I am missing. Perhaps you too have something that keeps bringing you to sorrow's doorstep, and you wonder what there could possibly be to celebrate.

Many times at a funeral, whoever is hosting the bereaved family at the church will provide a dinner for family and friends. In a sense, it might seem a little unusual for a grieving family to quickly move into celebration mode, because breaking bread with loved ones is usually a time of joy and camaraderie.

But this is the picture David gives us in Psalm 23:5. A table is spread out for the psalmist in this verse, and it is spread out "in the presence of my enemies." The psalmist is welcomed to enjoy a threefold blessing: a tableful of provisions, an anointing of oil, and a filled-to-overflowing cup.

God does not want us to be stuck in our sorrow or our pain. He shepherds us to move from trouble to triumph, as this verse suggests. He provides us with a table of food, reminding us that He is there to meet all of our needs. He pours on our heads the oil of anointing, or blessing, reminding us that we are still His children and will never be forsaken. And He makes our cup overflow with His love and understanding, reminding us that even in our tough times, He is our go-to Person.

To Be Content, I Need Support
"Goodness and love will follow me" (Psalm 23:6).

The first few days after we lost Melissa gave us a preview of how God would pour out His goodness and mercy on us in all of the years since. He put so many people in our lives to support us and encourage us and let us know that we were not alone!

Nothing spoke louder about the goodness and mercy that would follow us for our entire journey without our daughter than the number of people who gave up their Sunday to express their love at Melissa's visitation. For ten straight hours, we received people who wanted to tell us they cared and promised to pray for us and be there for us. The folks at the funeral home said they had never seen so many people at a visitation.

To this day, the goodness and mercy of the hundreds of people who came by to hug us and say goodbye to Melissa still brings both tears to my eyes and warmth to my heart.

And the goodness and mercy has not stopped. I think of Cindi, who sends us a card every year on Melissa's death day and on her birthday. I think of Mandy, who lets us know occasionally that she will never forget her high school buddy Melissa. I think of the people who never met Melissa but still tell us they care!

God sends people sometimes to do His work of lifting our hearts with goodness and showing us genuine love and mercy.

To Be Content, I Need Hope
"I will dwell in the house of the LORD forever" (Psalm 23:6).

Remember that hope we talked about from Romans 5:3–4?

Look at the next verse: "Hope does not put us to shame, because God's love has been poured out into our hearts through the Holy Spirit" (v. 5).

The rest of Romans 5 is a grand, eloquent explanation of the salvation that gives us our hope. It explains what Jesus went through in order to reconcile us to himself, so we could be "justified by his blood," as verse 9 tells us.

It is hard to imagine how there could be any person on earth who does not want to take this gift that God offers us (v. 15). I often think about how hard people work to create for themselves a trouble-free life. They want to have a home that is comfortable, and they want to avoid difficulties such as heavy debt, personal conflict, and illness.

In effect, these people are seeking contentment. They try to eliminate all things that will make them discontent, and they wear themselves out seeking what, they think, will make them content in this world.

Yet so many of these same people reject God's offer of eternal contentment. They listen to the gospel message in verses such as Romans 5:21, which says, ". . . so also grace might reign through righteousness to bring eternal life through Jesus Christ our Lord," and they say, "No, thank you."

Somehow they do not see that true and eternal contentment is what Jesus has offered to every person who trusts in Him.

Somehow they do not understand the implications of the final words of this great psalm, which say, "I will dwell in the house of the LORD forever" (Psalm 23:6). Maybe they have heard it over and over. Perhaps they even have Psalm 23 on a plaque in their house, but they miss its final point.

How sad it would be to miss this.

Someday, because of what Jesus did for us on the cross—so clearly explained in Romans 5—I will see my precious Melissa again. In heaven, I will again connect with her, with my sister, with my parents, and with so many others whose faith anchored for them a place in heaven.

But it would be a slight to our Savior if we did not note that Psalm 23:6 spells out the source of our truest and greatest contentment when we find ourselves on the other side.

Here is what it says: "Surely your goodness and love will follow me all the days of my life [a great promise that is similar to what Jesus said in John 10:10], and I will dwell in the house of the LORD forever."

That, my friend, is the climax of this grand and masterful psalm. With those final ten words, David reminds us of what will give us our ultimate joy and our forever happiness. Our contentment on earth will grow pale compared with our ecstasy of dwelling in God's house forever.

When that happens, we will live the Psalms life in a new and exciting way, experiencing without reservation and with total abandon the glory of God.

As we anticipate that wonderful day, let us enjoy in a refreshing new way the blessedness, the worship, the security, and the contentment of our earthbound life. Let us be like that tree planted by streams of water (Psalm 1:1–3)—flourishing and fruitful for God's glory.

Notes

Introduction
1. Ray Stedman, *Folk Psalms of Faith* (Ventura, CA: Regal Books), 1973.

Chapter 5
1. Derek Kidner, *Psalms 73–100: A Commentary* (Downers Grove, IL: IVP, 1975), 417–18.

Chapter 6
1. "Barnes' Notes," BibleHub, http://biblehub.com/commentaries/barnes/psalms/18.htm.
2. Kelli B. Trujillo, "After 50 Years in a Wheelchair, I Still Walk with Jesus," *Christianity Today* (July 28, 2017), www.christianitytoday.com/women/2017/july/joni-eareckson-tada-fifty-years-wheelchair-walk-jesus.html (accessed March 12, 2018).
3. "More Than Dreams: Muslims Coming to Christ through Dreams and Visions," *Lausanne World Pulse Archives* (January 2007), www.lausanneworldpulse.com/perspectives-php/595/01-2007 (accessed March 12, 2018).
4. Geoffrey W. Grogan, *Psalms* (Grand Rapids, MI: Eerdmans, 2008), 305.

Chapter 9

1. "Matthew Henry's Concise Commentary," Bible Hub, http://biblehub.com/commentaries/psalms/73-17.htm.
2. Ray Stedman, "The View from the Sanctuary," Daily Devotions (2006), https://www.raystedman.org/daily-devotions/psalms/the-view-from-the-sanctuary.
3. Derek Kidner, *Psalms 1–72: A Commentary* (Downers Grove, IL: IVP, 1975), 85.

Enjoy this book? Help us get the word out!

Share a link to the book or
mention it on social media

Write a review on your blog, on a retailer site,
or on our website (dhp.org)

Pick up another copy to share with someone

Recommend this book for your
church, book club, or small group

Follow Discovery House on
social media and join the discussion

Contact us to share your thoughts:

 @discoveryhouse    @DiscoveryHouse

Discovery House
P.O. Box 3566
Grand Rapids, MI 49501 USA

Phone: 1-800-653-8333
Email: books@dhp.org
Web: dhp.org